CHAMPION OF FREEDOM

Mohandas Gandhi

CHAMPION OF FREEDOM

Mohandas Gandhi

By KEM KNAPP SAWYER

MORGAN
REYNOLDS
PUBLISHING

Greensboro, North Carolina

Champion of Freedom: Mohandas Gandhi
Copyright © 2012 by Morgan Reynolds Publishing

Morgan Reynolds Publishing, Inc.
620 South Elm Street, Suite 387
Greensboro, NC 27406 USA

Library of Congress Cataloging-in-Publication Data

Sawyer, Kem Knapp.
  Champion of freedom : Mohandas Gandhi / by Kem Knapp Sawyer.
    p. cm.
  Includes bibliographical references and index.
  ISBN 978-1-59935-166-7 (alk. paper)
  1. Gandhi, Mahatma, 1869-1948--Juvenile literature. 2.
Statesmen--India--Juvenile literature. 3. Nationalists--India--Juvenile
literature. I. Title.
  DS481.G3S334 2012
  954.03'5092--dc22
  [B]

                              2010047904

Printed in the United States of America
First Edition

Book Cover and interior designed by:
Ed Morgan, navyblue design studio
Greensboro, N.C.

To Jon, and to all those who work for justice
and try to overcome evil with good

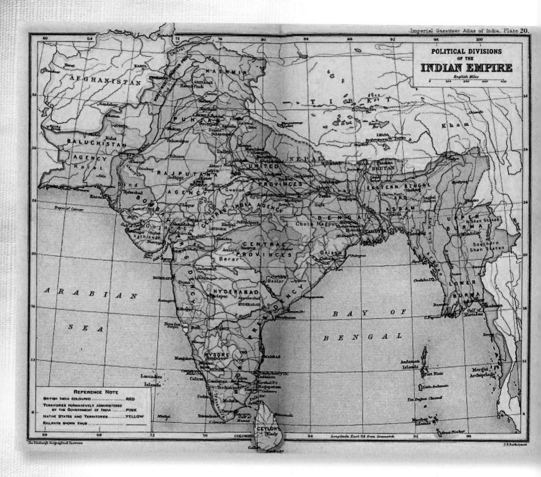

A 1909 map of the British Indian Empire,
from *The Imperial Gazetteer of India*

Table of Contents

CHAPTER ONE

Indian Roots

In high school, Mohandas Gandhi let a friend convince him to take a stand against British rule in their native India by doing something that Gandhi's family had strictly forbidden him to do: eat meat. The friend told Gandhi, "we are a weak people because we do not eat meat. The English are able to rule over us, because they are meat-eaters . . . . They know its virtues. You should do likewise. Try, and see what strength it gives."

Though Gandhi was only thirteen or fourteen at the time, he had strong views about the British presence in India, and he wanted to see reform in his country, as did many others. A popular poet named Marmad had penned a rhyme that Gandhi and his schoolmates liked to recite:

Behold the mighty Englishman
He rules the Indian small,
Because being a meat-eater
He is five cubits tall

Gandhi's meat-eating friend, Sheik Mehtab, was physically strong and athletic, excelling at long-distance running and high jumping. Gandhi considered himself weak and cowardly. He despised the dark and had to sleep with a light on. He was afraid of ghosts, snakes, and thieves. After continued coaxing from Mehtab—and learning that his older brother had started eating meat, too—Gandhi finally concluded that it was his duty to eat meat, believing that "it would make me strong and daring, and that, if the whole country took to meat-eating the English could be overcome." So one day, by a river, Mehtab gave Gandhi his first taste of meat—goat. Gandhi hated it. Nevertheless, for about a year, the teenager continued to secretly eat it, until the guilt of lying to his parents as well as his wife—Gandhi's parents had arranged for him to marry at age thirteen—got the best of him.

Gandhi gave up the eating of meat and vowed never to eat it while his parents were alive. But he didn't give up his conviction that British rule of India must end, and that youthful act was the beginning of many Gandhi would engage in to set his beloved country free.

Mohandas Karamchand Gandhi was born on the western coast of India in a city called Porbandar on October 2, 1869. His family was Hindu. Porbandar was an old city dotted with temples overlooking the Arabian Sea.

Mohandas's boyhood home was solidly built of limestone, three stories tall with walls twenty feet thick. Many rooms surrounded a courtyard—Mohandas's parents and brothers and sisters lived in two of them and various aunts, uncles, and cousins occupied the remainder.

The word "gandhi" means "grocer" in the Gujarati language, and the Gandhi family assumed their ancestors had been grocers. However, for several generations, the family had been engaged not in trade but in politics.

Mohandas's father Karamchand held the title of *diwan* (or prime minister) in the princely state of Porbandar. He reported to the prince, performed administrative duties, and was charged with settling disputes. Mohandas's grandfather had held the same post. Karamchand assumed one of his sons would carry on the tradition.

the british raj (1858 –1947)

India was part of the British Empire when Gandhi was born. This period of British control of India was called the British Raj. (Raj is the Hindi word for rule.) During the Raj, India was much larger than it is today. It extended over all regions of present-day India, Pakistan, and Bangladesh. At various times, it also included Burma (now Myanmar), the Colony of Aden, British Somaliland (today, an independent republic in the northern part of Somalia), and Singapore.

India was separated into provinces, the majority of which were controlled directly by the British, and "princely states." These were governed by Indian rulers who had entered into treaties of mutual cooperation with Great Britain. There were almost one thousand in-dependent principalities, or "princely states," during the early part of the twentieth century. In most cases, the local kings, or rulers, had inherited their throne and government from their fathers. Some of these states were small, others large—for example, Hyderabad was the size of England and Wales combined. Nizam, its ruler, was one of the richest men in the world.

The entire country of India was overseen by a viceroy sent from London. A viceroy served a five-year term and re-sided in Calcutta, that is until 1912, when the seat of government was moved to New Delhi.

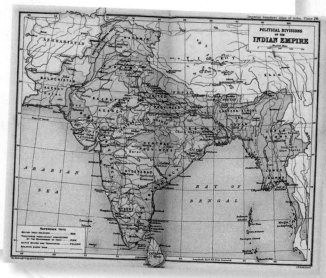

A 1909 map of the British Indian Empire, from *The Imperial Gazetteer of India*

Mohandas admired and respected Karamchand—considering him truthful and brave. Karamchand had received only a modest formal education, but he learned from experience. Widely respected, he was a fair and honest man with high principles. His biggest weakness was a short temper. Karamchand married four times. Mohandas was the youngest child of his fourth wife.

Putlibai, Mohandas's mother, was a teenager when she married her husband, then in his forties. To Mohandas she seemed saintly. Deeply religious, Putlibai prayed before every meal, visited the temple daily, and fasted throughout Chaturmas (the four-month rainy season)—vowing to eat only during the brief moments of sunshine. While it rained Mohandas and his siblings often stood outside waiting for the sun to appear. As soon as they saw the sun they rushed inside to tell their mother, but frequently, by the time she stepped outside the sun was no longer visible—and Putlibai would stand firm, refusing to take any food.

The Gandhis were Vaishnavas, a sect of Hinduism that worshipped a supreme deity—the god named Vishnu. They also followed traditions of Jainism, an ancient religion that originated in India. Jainists were taught that all living beings had souls and that no harm should be done to them. They were encouraged to lead a simple, pure life and to seek harmony and peace. Mohandas grew up to respect these beliefs.

The majority of Indians were Hindu. Not all Hindus adhered to the same rituals or had the same gods, but they all studied the same sacred scriptures and worshiped in ancient temples. A large minority of Indians were also Muslim—followers of Islam, a monotheistic religion. Their central beliefs were recorded in the Qur'an, a holy text that was revealed to the Prophet Muhammad in the seventh century.

Mohandas attended school in Porbandar. He was a weak student; multiplication tables proved particularly difficult to master. He learned more from his family than he did from his formal education. He was fond of animals and enjoyed listening to other people's conversations.

After serving in Porbandar for twenty-five years, Karamchand was appointed *diwan* in the court of Rajkot, 120 miles from Porbandar.

Mohandas Gandhi at the age of seven.

When Mohandas was seven, Putlibai and her children joined Karam-chand in Rajkot.

Mohandas moved on to Alfred High School where he was atten-tive, reasonably diligent, and always honest. He never became a stellar student and was so shy he seldom spoke to anyone. All classes were taught in English. During the education inspector's visit, the students were given a spelling test. Mohandas's teacher wanted them to do well so the inspector would think he was a good teacher. When he saw that Mohandas had misspelled the word "kettle," he nudged him with his boot and motioned for him to copy his neighbor's slate. Mohandas did not want to cheat. He was the only one in the class with an incor-rect spelling.

Mohandas's parents arranged for their son to marry at an early age—as was the custom in India. Mohandas was engaged twice before he turned seven but both girls died young. The third girl his parents chose was Kasturbai Majanki, the beautiful daughter of their neighbors in Porbandar. Her father was a merchant who sold cloth, cotton, and grain. Mohandas and his bride to be were both thirteen years old.

Hindu weddings are spectacular, expensive affairs that require months of preparation. Dresses are ornate, jewelry plentiful and meals are elaborate feasts with multiple courses, great variety, and abundant portions. In 1883, the Gandhi family decided to marry their middle son Karsandas, along with Mohandas and a cousin.

The triple wedding took place in Porbandar. Karamchand traveled by stagecoach from Rajkot—attempting to do in three days what was normally a five-day journey. As the stagecoach speeded along Karamchand was thrown from the coach. He suffered serious injuries, but the ceremony could not be delayed. Karamchand arrived at the wedding covered in bandages.

Mohandas and Kasturbai took part in the traditional ceremony—circling a fire and reciting the seven marriage vows. They promised each other to be strong, to live a healthy life, and to seek prosperity. They also pledged to pray for happiness, to serve others, to lead a religious life, and to remain loyal to each other. At the end of the ceremony they placed *kansar*—a mixture of crushed wheat and sugar—in each other's mouths.

Young newlyweds were expected to live with the groom's parents. The bride, however, would return to her parents' home for several months during the year. Kasturbai and Mohandas followed this tradition for the first five years of their marriage. When they lived under the same roof Mohandas was controlling, possessive and jealous. He became suspicious whenever Kasturbai left the house. Kasturbai stood up to him and did as she pleased. Still, although they bickered a great deal, they grew fond of each other.

Mohandas continued his high school education—struggling with geometry and Sanskrit, the ancient language of India. His handwriting was notably poor—he later concluded that all children would have better penmanship if they learned first to draw and then to write. Still shy as a teenager, Mohandas did not enjoy games such as cricket or football. For exercise he took long walks—a habit he kept up throughout his life.

It was during his high school years that Mohandas met Sheik Mehtab, his older brother's friend and classmate. Mohandas's mother,

Mohandas with his elder brother Laxmidas in 1886

older brother, and wife warned him that Sheik was "bad company." But Mohandas pleaded with them: "I know he has the weakness you attribute to him, but you do not know his virtues. He cannot lead me astray . . . . if he reforms his ways, he will be a splendid man."

Instead of reforming, though, Sheik led Mohandas to do all sorts of things he later regretted: smoking, going to a brothel, eating meat, and acting violently toward his wife.

Mohandas also stole a bit of gold from his brother. Overwhelmed with guilt he wanted to obtain his father's forgiveness. Only then could he forgive himself. Mohandas wrote a note to his father, confessing what he had done and promising never to steal again. He trembled as he handed his father the note. Karamchand read the note and said nothing. His eyes welled up with tears as he tore the paper in two. Mohandas had expected his father to show his anger—instead he was astounded by his father's love for him. After this episode, becoming virtuous or "moral" became an obsession with Mohandas. He sought the truth—wanting both to be truthful and to learn what was true. Mohandas was also learning the value of returning good for evil, something that would become increasingly important to him.

As for his friendship with Sheik, he later wrote that it was a "tragedy," and described that time in his young life as "dark days."

In 1885, Karamchand, now sixty-three years old, became ill and bedridden. Every day Mohandas would rush home from school to spend time with him. At night he would massage his father's legs. Karamchand's brother came to visit knowing it might be for the last time. Late one evening, as Mohandas was caring for his father, his uncle sent him to bed. He would watch over Karamchand.

Mohandas went to his room to join his wife. Minutes later the servant knocked at the door and told him his father had died. Mohandas wished he had not left his father's room—he felt that he had proved himself to be neither a dutiful nor worthy son. Kasturbai and Mohandas's first child was born shortly thereafter, but died after a few days. For the remainder of his life Mohandas would consider the loss of his baby's life a punishment for leaving his father's bedside.

After he finished high school Mohandas traveled to Ahmedabad, a large city not far from Rajkot, to take a college entrance examination. He passed and was admitted to Samaldas College.

The college courses proved too difficult and Mohandas returned home after one term to join Kasturbai and their new son, a healthy baby boy named Harilal, born while Mohandas was away at college.

Mavji Dave, an old family friend, paid a visit to the Gandhis to discuss Mohandas's future. He wanted Mohandas to follow his father's

A 1915 photograph of the front of the University College of London in Great Britain

footsteps and pursue a political career. However, first, Mohandas would need to prepare. He should go to England to study law at the University College of London and become a barrister. Going to England appealed to Mohandas. He would have preferred to study medicine, but Mavji insisted a legal background would better prepare Mohandas to become a *Diwan*.

Putlibai did not want her son to live so far away. She was concerned that he might fall into bad habits. Mohandas's uncle worried that Mohandas would adopt British dress and take up cigar smoking. Putlibai asked Becharji Swami, a Jainist monk, for guidance. Becharji Swami counseled the family to allow Mohandas to go—provided he make three promises. He must vow to remain faithful to his wife, to not eat meat, and to avoid alcohol. When Mohandas agreed to take these vows, Putlibai relented. Laxmidas, Mohandas's older brother, consented to finance the trip. Mohandas seemed to worry little about leaving his wife and baby son behind. He would pursue his education and return better prepared to support his family.

In June 1888, the seventeen-year old Mohandas left his home in Rajkot. He traveled first to Bombay (the city now called Mumbai) with plans to sail from there to England. But the rough weather made sailing dangerous. Mohandas was told he should postpone his ocean voyage. The news came as an unexpected blow. Mohandas wondered if he would ever set foot in England.

Jewel in the Crown

In 1858 British Crown rule was established in India, and India soon became known as the "Jewel in the Crown" of the vast British Empire. The American colonies had been seen as the jewel, but that changed after the British lost the colonies in 1783. There were several reasons why Benjamin Disraeli, the British prime minister from 1874 to 1881, called India "the brightest jewel in the crown." For one, the country was a great source of labor for the Empire. The British transported large numbers of Indians to its colonies all over the world—South Africa, Rhodesia (now Zimbabwe), Kenya, Fiji, Mauritius, Sri Lanka, the West Indies, Malaysia, etc.—to serve as farmers, laborers, and "coolies." India also helped the Empire maintain a large standing army at no cost to the British taxpayer.

Yet another economic benefit provided by India was its captive market for British goods and services. And perhaps most importantly, India was rich with sapphires, rubies, diamonds, emeralds, cotton, wheat, expensive spices, and other resources that the British sought to exploit.

An emerald crystal

CHAPTER TWO

To England and Back

Gandhi set sail for London on September 4, 1888. He had eagerly anticipated the voyage for months; once on board, however, he was filled with trepidation. He usually dined alone in his cabin and was reluctant to speak English to the other passengers even though he had learned it in school.

Gandhi was now five foot five and thin and paid careful attention to his appearance. His black hair was always neatly combed. He had bought British-style clothes before leaving India and had put aside a white flannel suit for his arrival. But, stepping off the boat at Southampton in late September, he felt out of place when he found no one else dressed in white. In spite of his embarrassment he was excited to have arrived in Britain, a country familiar to him only through textbooks.

The British had just finished a grand celebration of the Golden Jubilee—the fiftieth anniversary of Queen Victoria's accession to the throne. Their country was prospering; their monarch beloved.

Victoria ruled the world's greatest power and had taken the title of Empress of India. The theaters, music halls, and opera houses were packed. At the same time cities were overcrowded and thousands of people were living in squalor.

New sights, sounds, and smells overwhelmed Gandhi as he traveled from Southampton, where the boat docked, to London and checked into the Victoria Hotel. He had with him a letter of introduction to Dr. P. J. Mehta, who helped him adjust to the city. His newfound friend discussed clothing, food, and manners, and also helped him locate rooms in a house in West Kensington, a pleasant London neighborhood. Gandhi enjoyed the company of his landlady—a widow—and her two daughters, but he was homesick. He missed his family and his country—every night he cried himself to sleep.

The new and strange food was a problem. Gandhi liked the oatmeal porridge his landlady made in the morning, but lunch and dinner were never satisfactory. Because he didn't eat meat he ate the spinach and a few slices of bread that were put in front of him and left the table hungry.

For weeks Gandhi wandered the streets of London searching for a vegetarian restaurant he liked. Most offered dishes that tasted very bland. Finally, he found a hearty meal at a vegetarian restaurant on Farringdon Street, where he also found a book called *Plea for Vegetarianism* by Henry A. Salt. The book influenced him a great deal and led him to read others on the subject. The more he read the more convinced he became of the merits of vegetarianism.

Gandhi occasionally found it difficult to be accepted by all segments of British society. Still, he did his best to fit in. He read British newspapers. He bought new suits, a top hat, and ties. He asked his brother to send him a gold watch chain. He took lessons in French, elocution, and ballroom dancing (but had difficulty keeping time). He purchased a violin and started lessons.

After three months, Gandhi had second thoughts. He was spending many hours improving himself—but very little time learning the law. He worried about money and did not want to become indebted.

He weighed his options carefully and then made a conscious decision to give up his attempts to become a cultured gentleman. He would simplify his life and focus on his legal studies.

Abandoning his living arrangement in West Kensington, he found a suite of rooms within walking distance of the college. He saved money both on rent and transportation. Later he moved into one room. He started to cook more frequently and eat out less. He made his own breakfast of oatmeal and cocoa. He did go out for lunch, but he ordered frugally—returning home for a simple dinner of bread and cocoa.

Well aware that early marriages were frowned on in England, Gandhi was embarrassed to tell his new acquaintances that he had left a wife and son behind in India. When an older widow took a motherly interest in him and invited him to dine at her house every Sunday, he neglected to mention Kasturbai and Harilal. His hostess introduced him to several young ladies and tried to encourage a match. Gandhi had no interest in becoming entangled but worried about the best way to tell his hostess. He wrote many drafts of a letter before finally presenting her with his written explanation. Gandhi thought she might never want to see him again, but (much to his relief) she responded quickly and said that she understood—and would still expect him for Sunday dinner.

The study of religion also preoccupied Gandhi. He became acquainted with Theosophists, members of a group who sought to find common links between various religions. Reading and discussing the *Bhagavad Gita* with other Theosophists, he gained a deeper understanding of this sacred Hindu writing, the title of which means "song of God." Here the Hindu god Krishna talks about the meaning of life with the warrior Arunja. Krishna teaches him the value of detachment, selflessness, and self-purification. Arunja learns that one must seek the truth through both meditation and action. Only then can one find the greater good.

Gandhi also pored over the preaching of Jesus in the Bible's New Testament. The message of the Sermon on the Mount touched him profoundly. Jesus preaches to his disciples that if someone strikes you

The Sermon on the Mount, an 1890 oil painting by Danish-born artist
Carl Heinrich Bloch. The lessons from The Sermon on the Mount
greatly impressed young Gandhi as he studied other religions.

on one cheek, "turn to him the other also." As a young boy brought up
in the Hindu and Jainist faiths, Mohandas had learned to render good
for evil. Now, almost 4,000 miles from home, he found similarities in
the teachings of the two great religions of Hinduism and Christianity.

Gandhi's interests were wide and diverse: he read philosophy and
religion; he met people from different walks of life; he traveled to Paris.

Some of his time, of course, had to be devoted to the study of law. British students were expected to spend three years preparing at a university. Before they could serve as lawyers in court they would have to pass examinations in Roman Law and Common Law. However these exams were not rigorous. Gandhi observed that British students could pass without much effort—they often did not complete the readings, but spent only a couple weeks studying for the Roman Law exam and two or three months preparing for the Common Law exam. If students did not pass the first time they would be given three other opportunities during the year.

Not one to take any shortcuts, Gandhi read the entire texts that were assigned. After reading Roman law in Latin, as well as many volumes of English Common Law, he passed his exams. On June 10, 1891, he was called to the bar. The next day he enrolled in the High Court—he was now a barrister.

Gandhi had always intended to return to India to practice law. On June 12, 1891, he set sail for Bombay aboard the luxury steamship the *Oceana*. The first part of the journey went smoothly—he enjoyed the vegetable curries and other vegetarian fare. At Aden, a Yemeni port, Gandhi and the other India-bound passengers transferred to a smaller boat, the *Assam*. For the remainder of the journey, the sea was rough and most passengers—with the exception of Gandhi—suffered from seasickness. Gandhi was one of the few strong enough to remain on deck. Standing against the ship's railing, he watched the turbulent waves and planned for his homecoming.

Laxmidas waited at the dock in Bombay ready to greet his younger brother. He had tragic news. His mother had died. His family had wanted to wait until his return to inform him. Gandhi grieved for his mother—the memory of her compassion and religious devotion would remain with him forever.

Gandhi returned to Rajkot to be with his family. Before long he found his wife still brought out the old feelings of jealousy. Little had changed in their relationship. Kasturbai had never learned to read or write and his attempts to teach her failed. Gandhi did enjoy

teaching his son Harilal, now almost four, as well as his nephews. He also showed them the benefits of exercise, played, and joked with them. But there were no job opportunities in Rajkot. Gandhi, although qualified to practice law in England, knew little of Indian law and did not feel ready to take on a client in India—or charge him a fee.

Following a friend's advice, the young barrister moved to Bombay to study Hindu law. He attended the High Court as an observer,

A 1905 file photo of the University of Bombay Hall and Rajabai Tower, from *India Illustrated* magazine. The University of Bombay, now the University of Mumbai, is where Gandhi studied law.

and enjoyed the walk there and back (forty-five minutes each way), which helped him stay fit. Later he would attribute his good health to this exercise. In the midst of his studies Gandhi took on a case that was deemed of small consequence, one that should occupy no more than a day. But when it came time for Gandhi to speak he could not utter a word—he was tongue-tied. He had to sit down and could not continue. He later abandoned the case. While his client engaged another lawyer, Gandhi berated himself for his shyness and lack of courage.

Ready to abandon the practice of law, Gandhi applied for a teaching position, but was turned down. It was difficult to find employment so, after six months in Bombay, he returned to his household in Rajkot. He set up a small legal practice, drafting applications for clients but not appearing or speaking in court.

Laxmidas was eager for his younger brother to advance. He often found small jobs for him, but work was scarce. Obviously, he needed a change in his life. When Laxmidas presented him with a job opportunity in South Africa, Gandhi did not hesitate.

CHAPTER THREE

Setting the Stage

Abdulla Sheth, a Muslim Indian businessman, needed legal counsel in South Africa and had asked Laxmidas for a recommendation. Gandhi, looking for a way to support his growing family, agreed to take on the new client. Gandhi and Kasturbai were now the parents of two small children—the four-year old Harilal and a baby boy, the six-month old Manilal.

In April 1893, Gandhi traveled to Bombay leaving his wife and two sons in Porbandar. He found a ship ready to set sail for South Africa, but was told all the berths were taken—he would have to sleep on deck. Gandhi expected to travel first-class. He pleaded with the captain to find room for him. The captain finally relented and offered Gandhi the extra berth in his cabin. Gandhi and the captain enjoyed playing chess together and became friends. After stopping at several ports along the way they arrived at the port city of Durban in South Africa, at the end of May.

At the time South Africa was ruled by both the British and Dutch-speaking settler farmers known as Boers. The Dutch had arrived at the Cape of Good Hope, on the Atlantic coast of South Africa, in 1652.

After a series of frontier wars with the Khoikhoi (translated it means *men of men*) and Xhosa people who lived in the southern part of the country, they had taken control of much of the Cape. But in 1795 the British seized this territory, ending almost 150 years of Dutch rule. The British then ceded it to the Dutch in 1803, only to take it back again in 1806—calling it the Cape Colony. The British fought to hold on to the Cape, because they wanted to control the lucrative trade route to India that passed around the Cape.

The Boers migrated northeast to land that would become known as the Orange Free State and the Transvaal. Throughout the 1800s, the Boers and the British fought each other as well as other indigenous groups, including the Zulus, who occupied land in the south-east region of South Africa. The British defeated the Zulu Kingdom in 1879, and later annexed Zululand.

Two years later the British and the Boers fought the First Boer War over disputed territory. In the peace agreement of 1881, the British relinquished the Transvaal to the Boers. South Africa was now divided into four states: the Transvaal and the Orange Free State controlled by the Boers; Cape Colony and Natal governed by the British.

By the time Gandhi arrived in South Africa, more than 75,000 Indians had settled in the country and more than two thirds of them lived in Natal.

Indians first came to South Africa as indentured laborers to cultivate and harvest sugarcane in Natal, which later became known as the last British outpost. The *Truro* dropped anchor in Natal Bay on Friday the 16th of November 1860, with 340 Indian laborers on board. Five days later the *Belvedere* followed with 302. The local newspaper introduced the laborers with a banner headline: "The Coolies are Here."

Sugarcane was first produced in Natal in 1851, and the colony seemed set for a major economic boom. But the planters and landowners had a serious problem: the indigenous Zulus had no interest in toiling in the fields of the white sugar barons. The Zulus' lives revolved around a culture of cattle, and the Natalians, as they were known, had failed in their attempts to exploit them. So the plantation owners

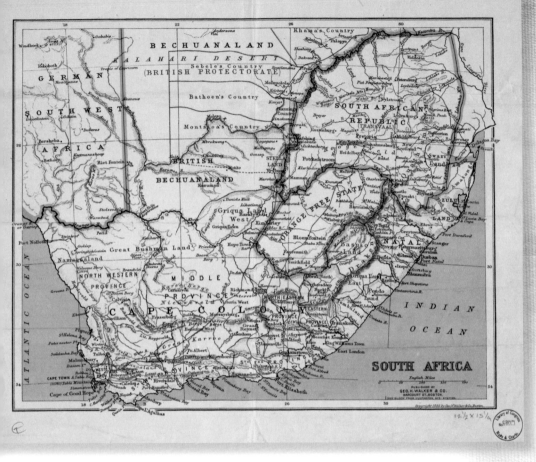

An 1899 map of South Africa

looked throughout the British Empire, and after lengthy and often bitter negotiations between the governments of Natal, Britain, and India, Indians from the slums of Madras and Calcutta began arriving in 1860.

Once on shore, armed police herded the immigrants into unfinished barracks, with no toilets, washing or cooking facilities. They remained under guard for eight days—four died during the wait—until their new masters came to collect them. The contract, or indenture, stipulated that a laborer would be assigned to a particular planter for three years (later amended to five years) and then be re-indentured, perhaps to the same planter, for another two years. After residence in Natal of a further five years as a "free" worker, the laborer had the choice of accepting free passage back to India or of remaining in Natal on a small grant of Crown land.

The laborers were given free room and board by their employer, and paid two shillings a month in the first year of service, rising annually by one shilling a month for the remainder of their contracts. Typically, workers began cutting the tall sugar cane before dawn, after a breakfast of cold porridge. They remained in the fields—planting, digging, breaking new soil, cutting, harvesting, carrying, and building—until the sun set. It was back-breaking work.

The white colonists regarded the "coolies" as units of labor—nothing more. A column in the local *Natal Witness* newspaper summed up their views:

> The ordinary Coolie . . . and his family cannot be admitted into close fellowship and union with us and our families. He is introduced for the same reason as mules might be introduced from Montevideo, oxen from Madagascar or sugar machinery from Glasgow. The object for which he is brought is to supply labour and that alone. He is not one of us, he is in every respect an alien . . .

Illiterate, cheap, frightened, and exploitable, Indian immigrants endured discrimination and oppression as part of their daily lives. But even with these harsh conditions, roughly 52 percent decided to remain in southern Africa after serving out their contracts. South Africa offered them opportunities—the possibility of a free life in a new country at the end of their servitude.

Not all Indians came to Natal as indentured laborers. "Passenger" merchants, also known as "Arabs," began to arrive in the 1870s. Most were Muslims from the state of Gujarat in India, and they brought considerable capital with them. They set up shops to sell to the indentured and ex-indentured Indians, as well as to Africans and whites. When members of this elite group, who were wealthy and ambitious, had grievances, they petitioned the colonial secretary in London. They complained of police brutality and harassment, and of a 9 o'clock curfew. By 1893, however—the year Gandhi arrived— their appeals to England or India were much less likely to succeed, because by then Natal had been granted its own self-government.

Meanwhile, resentment among white Natalians toward the affluent "Passenger," or "Arab" merchants, began to grow, and increasingly, they put pressure on Natal politicians to contain the "merchant menace." White fear that these "aliens" might demand greater political rights was also a driving force behind the anti-trader sentiment. It is for this reason that businessman Abdulla Sheth sought out Gandhi to represent him and his firm. Indian traders like Sheth had the resources to fight discrimination, and with the help of Gandhi, began dispatching an endless stream of petitions and memoranda to people in positions of authority.

Soon after Gandhi arrived in Durban, he began work on his lawsuit and went to court. Gandhi wore a frock coat, neat trousers, and a black turban—but the magistrate presiding over the court did not approve of Gandhi's turban. Only Indians who were Muslims were permitted to wear turbans. Gandhi left the court disappointed—he thought the turban commanded a certain amount of respect; he also did not like being told what not to wear. Undaunted, he continued to wear his turban. The incident over the turban was picked up in the press and the coverage helped Gandhi earn the reputation of a defiant young barrister.

Abdulla Sheth sent Gandhi to Pretoria, the capital of the Transvaal, to represent his trading company. Gandhi's employer accompanied him to the train station in Durban and bought him a first-class ticket. Gandhi boarded the train. This trip to Pretoria would turn out to be one of the most critical experiences in his life.

Mohandas Gandhi during the early years of his legal practice

Only the wealthy rode first-class—the cars were comfortable and clean. As Gandhi boarded the train and took his seat, he prepared to admire the scenery—assuming an enjoyable journey lay ahead.

At the next station stop his plans for a pleasant trip were ended. A passenger of European descent opened the door to Gandhi's compartment and looked at him disapprovingly. He did not expect to share the compartment with a person of color. When he saw that Gandhi was not going to give up his seat he went off in search of the train conductor.

The man returned with two railway officials who stood at the door without speaking and waited for Gandhi to leave. He kept his seat.

Next the chief conductor entered the compartment and asked Gandhi to move to the third-class compartment. But again he did not leave his seat. The conductor insisted—Gandhi did not move.

When the conductor told him he was going to summon the police Gandhi answered, "I refuse to get out voluntarily."

A policeman was called. As soon as he arrived he pushed Gandhi off the train. He stood alone on the platform and watched the train depart the station.

Gandhi spent a long, cold night in the waiting room. The experience had shaken him to the core. He could not sleep. During the early hours of the morning he contemplated his future. He considered returning to India but then thought better of it—he did not want to admit defeat.

If Mohandas Gandhi went on to Pretoria, he would still be faced with choices. He could proceed with his work and act as if nothing had happened. But dismissing what had happened would be the same as accepting it. Alternatively, he could fulfill his obligations to his employer while at the same time refusing to ignore the treatment he had received. Gandhi made the more difficult and daring choice. He later reflected, "The hardship to which I was subjected was superficial—only a symptom of the deep disease of color prejudice. I should try, if possible, to root out the disease and suffer hardships in the process."

When Gandhi arrived in Pretoria, a visiting American told him about the Johnston's Family Hotel, after overhearing a ticket collector tell Gandhi that he couldn't help him find a place to stay. The hotel keeper, also an American, agreed to let him stay one night, but told him only whites were allowed to eat in the dining room. Gandhi would have to take his dinner in his room. However, that evening Mr. Johnston knocked on Gandhi's door and invited him to come down to the dining room. "I was ashamed of having asked you to have your dinner here," Johnston said. "So I spoke to the other guests about you. . . . They said they have no objection." Johnston added, "please . . . stay here as long as you wish."

Everywhere Gandhi went in Pretoria he found restrictions placed on Indians. They were required to pay a fee to enter the Transvaal; they could not go outside after 9 pm without a permit; they were expected to walk on the street—public footpaths were not made accessible to them. Gandhi, however, refused to walk on the street and, as part of his daily routine, walked along a public footpath by the president's house. For many weeks the police did not trouble him. But then one policeman, new to the job, took the regulation to heart. When he saw Gandhi on the footpath he kicked him and shoved him onto the street. Gandhi changed his route after the assault, but he did not forget the insult.

Similar experiences led Gandhi to call a meeting of other Indians to discuss how they were treated in the Transvaal. Hindu, Muslim, Parsi, and Christian Indians gathered to hear him give his first public speech. Gandhi first spoke of the importance of being truthful and honest in business and then turned to the hardships they all faced in South Africa. He believed that Indians could best address these problems if they recognized their common identity, forgetting distinctions such as Hindus, Gujaratis, Punjabis, Suratis, Sindhis, and Madrasis, among others.

That first meeting went well and other meetings soon followed. Before long, there was not an Indian living in Pretoria that Gandhi did not know. And understanding the harsh conditions in which Indians lived prompted Gandhi to take other actions. He met with the British agent in Pretoria, and working with railway authorities, achieved one concession: Indians who were properly dressed could now purchase first- and second-class tickets. It was hardly a full-scale victory, but Gandhi's time in Pretoria would prepare him for future battles.

While alone in South Africa, far away from friends and family, Gandhi met several Christians who piqued his curiosity about religion. He read several books on Christianity and frequently engaged his new friends in long conversations. He found much to admire in Christianity but refuted his friends' claim that only those who accepted Christianity could find salvation.

Gandhi read the newly translated English edition of Leo Tolstoy's *The Kingdom of God Is Within You*. In the book Tolstoy discusses the Sermon on the Mount—Christ's commandment to "love your enemies, do good to those who hate you, bless those who curse you, pray for those who mistreat you. If someone strikes you on one cheek, turn to him the other also." Gandhi was deeply moved by the profound implications of the Sermon on the Mount and "the infinite possibilities of universal love." A longtime admirer of the writings of American Quakers, Tolstoy opposed all use of force and believed that nonresistance was a powerful weapon. War should be avoided at all costs. "True nonresistance is the one true resistance to evil. It kills and finally destroys the evil sentiment," he wrote. "They who take the sword perish with the sword, and those who seek peace, who act in a friendly manner, inoffensively, who forget and forgive offenses, for the most part enjoy peace, or, if they die, die blessed." Tolstoy shared the pacifist views of the Quakers, as well as their sense of belonging not to a nation but to the world.

Tolstoy was disturbed to see that for centuries the Christian Church had condoned the use of war. He believed that Christians were not practicing Christ's teaching. Questioning why Christians were willing to take part in war, Tolstoy wrote that even great men who look for truth see only what they want to see. "Slavery was contrary to all the moral principles which were preached by Plato and Aristotle, and yet neither the one nor the other saw this, because the negation of slavery

Tolstoy at his desk

destroyed all that life which they lived. The same happens in our world." Similarly violence is allowed not because it is necessary, but because "it has existed for a long time" and is practiced by men in power who "cannot tear themselves away from it."

Gandhi came to realize that there was much of Christianity that he wanted to embrace, and yet he also recognized its imperfections—the acceptance of violence by the leaders of the church. As he delved more deeply into Hinduism he also saw what he considered its flaws—the discrimination and abuse perpetuated by the caste system.

For centuries Indians had been divided into five castes, or inherited social groupings that determined a person's standing within the community. A Hindu was expected to marry a person belonging to the same caste. Originally the division of castes was based on occupation, but over time this distinction was lost. However, the caste system maintained its social hierarchy. The Brahmins (formerly priests) made up the highest caste; immediately below them were the Kshatriyas (formerly soldiers and government officials). Gandhi belonged to the third-highest caste, the Vaisyas (formerly tradespeople and farmers). Below them were the Sudras—or the working class. At the bottom of the caste system were the "untouchables." They performed the most menial tasks, were never allowed to mix with other castes, and endured harsh discrimination.

The segregation of the untouchables had shocked Gandhi from the time he was a young boy. As he grew older he became even more troubled—he wanted all people to be treated equally. He believed the divisions in society caused pain and suffering. Friends asked him to be patient, look beyond the caste system, examine the sacred texts, and come to understand the Hindu vision of the soul. As Gandhi pondered their words he remained open to all religions—concluding no one religion was perfect, but that he could learn from all faiths.

An Indian man from the caste of the untouchables
removes human excrement from the streets.

Gandhi believed that one should not try to convert others, but
that "our innermost prayer should be that a Hindu should be a better
Hindu, a Muslim a better Muslim and a Christian a better Christian."
He explained, "Religions are different roads converging to the same
point. What does it matter that we take different roads so long as we
reach the same goal?"

This study of religions did not keep Gandhi from his legal case.
He prepared diligently for it—reading papers, translating correspondence, investigating the facts. He concluded that the case involving

his client Abdulla Sheth and his opponent, Tyeb Sheth (his client's relative) could take months, if not years, to be resolved. The costs would rise accordingly and become prohibitive—to both parties. Gandhi persuaded Abdulla Sheth and Tyeb Sheth to consider arbitration—negotiations directed by a third party. They agreed and an arbitrator was appointed. Abdulla Sheth was awarded a large sum which Gandhi arranged for Tyeb Sheth to pay in installments. Gandhi felt that he had succeeded by finding a solution that would satisfy both sides. "The true function of a lawyer was to unite parties riven asunder," he said.

With the case behind him, Gandhi prepared to return home. But, at the farewell party Abdulla Sheth gave in his honor Gandhi learned that the House of Legislature had prepared a bill that would deprive Indians of their right to elect members to the Natal legislature. The guests pleaded with Gandhi to stay one more month and help them fight the bill. Gandhi agreed to delay his departure.

Petitions signed in protest of the bill were distributed and published, but, in spite of their work, the bill passed. The Indian community did not give up but renewed their efforts to claim their rights. Gandhi stayed on and started a new petition drive to oppose the bill. In two weeks he and his co-workers obtained 10,000 signatures. Gandhi requested no payment for his time, only funds to cover his expenses.

Gandhi settled into a house and prepared to practice law while continuing his public service. He applied for admission to the Supreme Court, the highest court in Natal. A person of color had never before been admitted but Gandhi succeeded and became the first Indian to do so. As he was being sworn in, he was asked to remove his turban and to adopt the dress worn by the other barristers. Gandhi acquiesced, later writing, "I wanted to reserve my strength for fighting bigger battles. I should not exhaust my skill as a fighter in insisting on retaining my turban. It was worthy of a better cause." Gandhi said he had learned to appreciate "the beauty of compromise."

In 1894, Gandhi and other Indian settlers established a formal party—the Natal Indian Congress. As leader, he took charge of the financial accounts and encouraged all members to participate. The Congress stood up for the rights of indentured servants and campaigned for lower taxes.

Three years passed before Gandhi returned to India. During this time he overcame much of his shyness. Yet he rarely spoke unless he had something to say. He was not afraid to take a stand or to bear the consequences. He did what he believed was right and cared little what others thought of him.

In July 1896, Gandhi set sail for India. He planned to bring his family back to South Africa. While at sea, he played chess with the captain and studied Urdu, the language of Muslim Indians, and Tamil, spoken in the southeast of India. Now deeply committed to improving the lives of Indians, Gandhi wanted to learn as many of their languages as he could.

In India, Gandhi reconnected with his family. He also cared for his brother-in-law, who was ill. He found nursing the sick very rewarding. "Such service can have no meaning unless one takes pleasure in it," he said. In spite of Gandhi's best efforts his brother-in-law died.

In order to spread the word on the conditions of Indians in South Africa, Gandhi wrote and published the *Green Pamphlet* (named for its green cover). Ten thousand copies were printed and widely distributed. He traveled throughout the country to gain support for his cause. He visited Bombay, Poona (like Bombay, a city situated in the west of the country), Madras in the south, and Calcutta, the capital of India during British rule.

Gandhi could successfully deliver a clear message to a small group; however he still had difficulties talking to a large group. His voice was naturally soft. When he spoke before a crowded hall in Bombay, he started to tremble. When urged to speak louder his voice only grew more inaudible. He finally handed his speech to a friend who was more comfortable speaking publicly. The audience listened intently.

Gandhi persevered and, by the time he reached Madras, had gained more confidence. He managed to deliver his speech in its entirety to a captivated audience.

In December 1896, the Indians in South Africa called on Gandhi to represent their cause in the new session of the Natal Indian Congress. Abdulla Sheth agreed to provide free passage for Gandhi and his family. Kasturbai and both of their sons, nine-year old Harilal and five-year old Manilal, would accompany him as well as his widowed sister's ten-year old son. Before their departure Gandhi advised his family on the proper dress and manners. He was most concerned that they create a good impression when they arrived in South Africa. Kasturbai wore a silk sari, which Gandhi considered the most refined of Indian dress. The boys wore knee-length coats and trousers and they all wore stockings and shoes. Although it was hard to become accustomed to some of the new clothes the family adapted well and did not complain.

Kasturbai Gandhi in South Africa (circa 1896)

The boat traveled directly from Bombay to Natal—but it was not an easy journey. The eighteen days the passengers spent at sea were rough. Terrible storms made them both anxious and nauseous. Gandhi, again one of the few who escaped seasickness, helped nurse and comfort the other travelers. He could not afford to become ill—he would need all his strength to meet the challenges that would face him once he landed in South Africa.

CHAPTER FOUR

Self-Reliance

As the passengers prepared to disembark in Durban, Gandhi learned that the white residents, fearing his arrival and the changes that would bring, had gathered to stage a protest. Rumor had it that Gandhi's life was in danger. His friends wanted him to slip away by coach to a safe house, but F. A. Laughton, a paid, white legal adviser but also a friend to the Indians, did not want him to give into fear and preferred that he go by foot. "I do not at all like the idea of your entering the city like a thief in the night," he said. Gandhi agreed and sent Kasturbai and the children ahead.

As soon as Gandhi stepped onto the dock, the crowd recognized him and yelled "Gandhi" in angry voices. The shouting grew louder. Within minutes he was being hit with stones, bats, and rotten eggs. The protesters kicked him, beat him, and tried to tear off his turban. Gandhi felt faint. The wife of the police superintendent, R. C. Alexander, approached him and opened her parasol to fend off the crowd.

Daily dockside protests, and government quarantine regulations, kept
Gandhi and eight hundred other Indian passengers on board a ship in the
Durban harbor for almost a month. When Gandhi finally disembarked,
protesters assaulted him until the Durban police commissioner's wife took
him to her home. The demonstrators later gathered outside the house,
chanting "We'll hang old Gandhi from the sour apple tree."

An Indian youth alerted the police. They sent a posse to escort
Gandhi to the safe house where his family waited. Later that night he
was taken in disguise to the police station so that he could receive better protection.

Gandhi was asked to press charges, but he refused. He explained
that nothing would come of prosecuting the assailants. They had been
told that Gandhi had made false claims about the whites in Natal. His
statements had been exaggerated and, Gandhi believed, it was the lies
that had frightened them. When they learned the truth, they would
regret their actions—that in itself would be punishment.

After his family was settled into their house, Gandhi continued the work he was becoming increasingly committed to pursuing. He opposed legislation that would restrict Indian immigration or discriminate against Indians. He also devoted time to nursing the sick—serving in a hospital for two hours a day.

Two more children were born to Kasturbai and Gandhi: a third son named Ramdas in 1897 (the year following their arrival in Natal), and three years later, a fourth son Devdas. This baby came so quickly that there was no time to fetch a doctor. It was Gandhi who safely delivered him. Gandhi had lived apart from his family when his first two sons were very young, but now he enjoyed watching over his infant sons.

Gandhi planned for his children, once they became adults, to take over the work he had started. He would not consider sending his children back to India for their schooling as some Indians in South Africa did, preferring to tutor them himself. He wanted his children to speak Gujarati, his native language, as well as English. He hired an English governess, but was not pleased with her and dismissed her after several months. The boys never received a typical education, but learned from "the school of experience" and "constant contact" with their parents. Later, Gandhi regretted that their exposure to academics was so limited.

As his sons grew older Gandhi was not able to give them the attention they needed. He tried hard to instill in them a sense of morality and explained what he thought was the most important and fundamental part of an education: "A child, before it begins to write its alphabet and to gain worldly knowledge, should know what the soul is, what truth is, what love is, what powers are latent in the soul. It should be an essential of real education that a child should learn, that in the struggle of life, it can easily conquer hate by love, untruth by truth, violence by self-suffering."

When Gandhi first brought his family to South Africa he tried to show them how successful he had become. But as he spent more time in South Africa he found himself less interested in possessions. He tried to simplify his lifestyle and cut back on expenses. He gave up visits to the barber and began cutting his own hair. He stopped sending his clothes to a washerman and cleaned and ironed them himself—teaching Kasturbai to do the same. Increasingly, he wanted to become more self-reliant.

Gandhi often provided housing for his law clerks until they were ready to strike out on their own. Since there were no servants to clean the chamberpots the clerks were supposed to take care of their own. But one clerk did not. Kasturbai cleaned it begrudgingly. Gandhi thought she should do so cheerfully and scolded her. Kasturbai shouted back at him and Gandhi then took her by the hand, led her away from the house, and pushed her out the gate. Tears streamed down her face as she cried, "Have you no sense of shame? . . . For Heaven's sake behave yourself, and shut the gate. Let us not be found making scenes like this!" Gandhi came to his senses and stopped arguing. As time passed he would bicker less.

In 1899, the Second Boer War broke out in South Africa. Once again the Boers and the British were fighting over the control of the Transvaal and the Orange Free State. Gandhi sympathized with the Boers but felt that since Indians were demanding to share the same rights as British citizens he and other Indians owed their allegiance to the British. Gandhi had always opposed the use of violence—yet, if the war had to be fought, he felt he needed to play his part. Although he greatly admired Tolstoy's philosophy he had not yet embraced pacifism. Thinking pragmatically of Indian rights, he could see there was much to gain by winning the approval of the British. To many of Gandhi's supporters his decision to join in the war effort seemed inconsistent with his personal philosophy, but to Gandhi the choice was clear. If he was in no position to stop the war from being fought, then he must support the war effort.

Gandhi brought together 1,100 Indians from various castes and from different ethnic and religious groups—indentured as well as free, to form an ambulance corps. At first the British refused their help, but eventually acquiesced. The corps worked for six weeks both within and outside the firing line. They risked their own lives as they walked twenty-five miles a day, carrying the wounded on stretchers.

During the war, more than 75,000 British, Boers, Africans, and Indians were killed. Peace came in 1902 when the Transvaal and the Orange Free State were made part of the British Empire. The British presented Gandhi with a war medal to show their gratitude.

The development of the ambulance corps did much to improve relations between the Indians and the British. Gandhi was ready to return home and be of service to India. His friends in South Africa agreed to let him go on one condition: he must come back to South Africa if he was needed. "The voice of the people is the voice of God, and here the voice of friends was too real to be rejected. I accepted the condition and got their permission to go."

Sorry to see the Gandhis leave and grateful for all they had done, the Indians in Natal wanted to give Gandhi and his family farewell gifts—gold watches and diamond rings. Gandhi believed that public servants should not accept expensive presents—"service was its own reward." Besides he had no desire to keep "costly ornaments" in the house. Kasturbai, on the other hand, resisted parting with them. After a sleepless night Gandhi decided he must confront his family. He suggested selling the gifts to create a fund that would serve the community. His children readily agreed. Kasturbai was still not convinced—she argued that the jewelry could be passed on to her future daughters-in-law. Gandhi and his sons persisted until Kasturbai was forced to relent.

In October 1901, the Gandhis returned to India and settled in Rajkot. Gandhi, however, did not stay long. He spent a month in Calcutta (the city in western Bengal, now called Kolkata) where he held meetings with leaders to discuss the conditions and rights of Indians living in South Africa. On a journey east to Burma he met with Buddhist monks. Traveling throughout India by train, he visited many places he had never seen. Gone were the days when he wished he could travel first-class; now he preferred third. He wanted to share the experience of those who were less wealthy and at the same time draw attention to the appalling conditions—both unsanitary and uncomfortable. He would campaign to improve these conditions and vowed never to let the railway authorities "rest in peace."

Less than a year passed before Gandhi received a cable summoning him back to South Africa. He kept his promise and once again returned to South Africa. He traveled to the Transvaal where he found that, as in Natal, Indians faced discrimination and struggled daily with injustice. The police system was corrupt—officers were easily bribed and did not treat Indian immigrants fairly.

A merchant friend helped Gandhi set up a law office in Johannesburg, the largest city in the Transvaal. Gandhi was admitted to the Transvaal Supreme Court and took on cases to support Indian rights. In June 1903, he started a journal to air the grievances of his people. The first issues of *Indian Opinion* were translated into Gujarati, English, Hindi, and Tamil. Albert West, an English friend with whom Gandhi often dined at a vegetarian restaurant, volunteered to manage the printing operation out of Durban.

Gandhi not only financed the publication, but he wrote weekly columns. He expounded on his theories of social justice, and discussed issues related to education, health, and vegetarianism. He included articles by important thinkers, authors and educators, such as Leo Tolstoy, or Booker T. Washington, who had suffered discrimination in the United States. Readers sent numerous letters reflecting a great variety of views—none of them went unanswered.

Gandhi wrote about his personal search for truth. He was convinced he could only find it through selflessness and service for others. As a follower of ahimsa (or nonviolence), he believed he must "hate the sin and not the sinner" and he taught others to do the same. He was ready to make more personal sacrifices, giving up not only luxuries but also basic comforts. He also adopted what he considered a healthier lifestyle—eating less and abandoning the use of medicines.

When Albert West ran into problems with the production of the journal, he asked Gandhi for help. Gandhi set out by train for Durban and brought with him the book *Unto This Last*—a gift from a friend.

The journey lasted twenty-four hours but Gandhi never slept. He was too busy reading *Unto This Last*. John Ruskin, a renowned British art critic, had spent the latter part of his life writing on politics, ethics, and the economy. He developed an anti-capitalist world view and wrote that all people had a right to earn their livelihood. The work of one man, who might be a lawyer, had the same value as that of another, who might be a barber. Ruskin stressed that laborers, such as the tillers of soil or craftsmen, led a "life worth living."

An artist's sketch of John Ruskin

Throughout his life Gandhi had little time for reading, but the books he did read were often transformative. *Unto This Last* was one of them. Gandhi took Ruskin's message to heart. He made plans to find a farm where he and the entire staff of the *Indian Opinion* could live and work. He wanted everyone to receive the same wage regardless of color, nationality, or job. Gandhi could be very persuasive. He had no trouble convincing most of the staff at the *Indian Opinion* to support his idea. Then he set out in search of land.

Albert West and Gandhi purchased one hundred acres in Phoenix, a town fourteen miles from Durban. Most of the land was overgrown and part of it covered with orange and mango trees. Gandhi hired carpenters to build living quarters for the staff—as well as a shed to house the press. Everyone put in long hours to build the settlement and at the same time produce the weekly paper. Several of Gandhi's relatives from India joined the group. Soon six families were living at the settlement—farming the land and sharing in the work.

Gandhi would have liked to spend all his time at the settlement but his law practice called him back to Johannesburg. Now that he would be staying in South Africa, Kasturbai and the three youngest boys moved to Johannesburg. Harilal stayed behind in India. Once again Gandhi neglected his sons' formal education. However, he often insisted the boys join him on his daily walks, and he used this time to instruct them.

In June 1906, a Zulu chief named Bambatha led a six-week rebellion against the British in Natal, after the British imposed a new poll tax, on top of existing hut and dog taxes, which in effect would have forced all Zulu men over the age of eighteen to work in the white farming and mining industries. Although Gandhi later said that he bore no grudge against the Zulus, he supported the British cause. Gandhi had been taught that the British Empire "existed for the welfare of the world"—his loyalty to the Crown remained deep-seated.

Gandhi volunteered to form an Indian Ambulance Corps to support the British army in Natal. His offer was immediately accepted. The family closed their house in Johannesburg and Gandhi left for the battlefront. Kasturbai and the boys settled in Phoenix.

Gandhi's house at the Phoenix settlement in South Africa

Gandhi's Mixed Messages

During the Bambatha-led rebellion Gandhi's sympathies were with the Zulus. In his autobiography he wrote: "My heart was with the Zulus, and I was delighted . . . to hear that our main work was to be the nursing of the wounded Zulus."

However, for most of his years in South Africa, Gandhi was so busy championing the cause of Indians he took little, or no, notice of the suffering of the black African majority. In later writings Gandhi expresses what modern interpreters consider no less than contempt, and, in some instances, outright racist views toward Africans in South Africa. In a March 7, 1908, article in the *Indian Opinion*, he wrote about sharing a prison cell with black convicts: "Kaffirs are as a rule uncivilized—the convicts even more so. They are troublesome, very dirty and live almost like animals." Kaffir is a South African pejorative. He also wrote, "Many of the native prisoners are only one degree removed from the animal and often created rows and fought among themselves."

When a statue of Gandhi was unveiled in Johannesburg in 2003, critics attacked the gesture for overlooking such statements by Gandhi. They said the British-trained barrister ignored the plight of Africans during his twenty-one years in the country, while defending Indians against racist laws.

But others, such as Nelson Mandela, South Africa's first black president, welcomed the eight-foot bronze statue in Gandhi Square in central Johannesburg. And historians credit Gandhi for forming South Africa's first organized political resistance movement, which inspired black South Africans to organize against legally institutionalized segregation known as apartheid.

Gandhi (middle row, fifth from the left) with the Indian Ambulance Corps during the Second Boer War in South Africa between 1899 and 1900

The British used machine guns and cannon to fight a people armed with spears—killing more than 3,000 Zulus. Once again Gandhi cared for the wounded, many of them Zulu, and he marched across many hills bearing a stretcher. He wrote later that during the long treks he was overwhelmed by the senselessness and "horrors of war." He did not know how to put a stop to it, but he re-affirmed his need to serve humanity. Now he would do so "with his whole soul."

Recognizing that his family took time away from his more important calling, Gandhi wanted to distance himself from these responsibilities so that he could devote himself to the needs of the community. He thought this dedication to others and service to humanity would only be possible through brahmacharya—the act of renouncing material things as well as sensual pleasure. This involved celibacy, which had been practiced for centuries by many Hindus seeking spiritual fulfillment.

Gandhi cared deeply for Kasturbai and wanted to share his life with her. She would continue to be "a helpmate, a comrade and a partner," he told her, and they would live together as brother and sister.

In 1906, at the age of thirty-seven, Gandhi took the vow of brahmacharya and he encouraged others to do the same. Some followed suit while others refused. Gandhi remained steadfast in his resolve. He later reflected that both he and Kasturbai had experienced "a life of contentment."

Brahmacharya

After taking his vow of celibacy, Gandhi spent the rest of his life trying to control his libido. He experimented with various diets, including one of fruits and nuts, that he believed would reduce his sexual urges. He tried other experiments as well, but some of his followers and family members found these "experiments" in self-restraint troubling. For example, in his last years Gandhi slept naked next to teenage girls, most notably his nineteen-year-old great-niece and constant companion, Manu. Gandhi has been criticized for not considering the negative psychological impact his behavior may have had on young girls. When questioned about this practice, Gandhi defended it, saying the perfect brahmachari was a man who could "lie by the side even of a Venus in all her naked beauty without being physically or mentally disturbed."

CHAPTER FIVE

Satyagraha in South Africa

The British, who wanted to stop Indian immigration to South Africa, tried to place as many restrictions as possible on Indian settlers. In 1906, the British published a draft of the new Asiatic Law Amendment Ordinance. Gandhi "saw nothing in it except hatred of Indians." All Indians—men, women, and children over eight—were to obtain a certificate from the Registrar of Asiatics. The applications were to include thumb or finger impressions. Those who failed to apply could be fined, deported, or imprisoned. Police officers would be allowed to enter houses to inspect certificates and no government services would be rendered unless a certificate was shown.

Convinced that this ordinance was only the first step the British would use to remove Indians from South Africa, Gandhi wanted to take immediate action. He organized a planning meeting to discuss options. On September 11, 1906, the delegates resolved not to submit to the ordinance and took a pledge not to register if it was passed. Their resistance would be nonviolent. Gandhi spoke to the large assembly of delegates telling them that the struggle would be difficult—those who took the pledge would risk going to jail. They might suffer from hunger, cold and heat, hard labor, heavy fines, deportation, and other hardships. He warned that those who fell back on their pledges would prolong the struggle, but "so long as there is even a handful of men true to their pledge, there can only be one end to the struggle, and that is victory." The delegates agreed to take the pledge—and many more Indians throughout the Transvaal did the same.

Gandhi needed a name for his movement. Nothing like it had ever been tried in South Africa. "Passive resistance" was not acceptable— Gandhi preferred a non-English term and wanted to steer clear of the word "passive" because it might connote weakness. His cousin Maganlal Gandhi suggested *sadagraha*—meaning "firmness in a good cause." This inspired Gandhi to think of satyagraha, a word composed of *satya* (love) and *agraha* (firmness). To Gandhi and his followers the term would come to mean the force which is born of truth, love, and non-violence. The word would become a call to take action and to combat injustice without resorting to violence.

"A Satyagrahi must never forget the distinction between evil and the evil-doer. He must not harbor ill-will or bitterness against the latter," Gandhi wrote. "A Satyagrahi will always try to overcome evil by good, anger by love, untruth by truth."

Gandhi's actions did not prevent passage of the ordinance by the legislature. The British agreed to only one modification: women would not be required to obtain registration certificates. The satyagrahis (as those who practiced satyagraha were called) sent Gandhi and H. O. Ali, a Muslim Indian businessman active in the movement, to England to meet with the British Committee of the Indian National Congress. They also called on members of Parliament and Lord Elgin, the secretary of state for the colonies. After six weeks Gandhi and H. O. Ali returned to South Africa uncertain of the outcome. On the voyage back they received a cable from Lord Elgin stating that he would advise the King not to put the ordinance into effect. Their journey was a success.

However, as soon as Gandhi and Ali arrived in Johannesburg, they learned they had been tricked. Lord Elgin would disallow the ordinance as long as the Transvaal was a Crown Colony—but the ordinance would be reinstated when the Transvaal legislature, composed of whites, took over the government. This transition would happen quickly so Gandhi and Ali's victory was short-lived.

Gandhi and others spoke out against the re-enactment of the ordinance. "Every Indian knows what the Black Act [the name given to the ordinance by the Indians] is and what it implies. . . . We know how powerful the Transvaal Government is. But it cannot do anything more than enact such a law. It will cast us into prison, confiscate our property, deport us or hang us. All this we will bear cheerfully, but we cannot simply put up with this law," Ahmad Muhammad Kachhalia, a satyagraha leader, said.

On July 1, 1907, the day the ordinance was reinstated, the satyagrahis picketed the permit offices. They continued their protest for several months and handed out literature explaining the consequences of the Black Act. They asked Indians to politely refuse to apply for a registration certificate. Protesters were told to treat police with respect and "suffer peacefully" if they were abused. The campaign was a success: of the 13,000 Indians who lived in the Transvaal, only five hundred completed the registration process.

Officials from the Asiatic Department arrested Gandhi and other prominent leaders of the protest and ordered them to leave the Transvaal. But the arrests did not have the desired effect. The satyagrahis refused to leave the Transvaal and pleaded guilty in court. Gandhi wanted to draw more attention to the issue and asked to receive the heaviest penalty. He was given a lighter sentence than he requested—the judge ruled that Gandhi and the other satyagraha leaders would serve two months in the Johannesburg prison.

Before long more than 150 satygraha volunteers were arrested and imprisoned. They were allowed no exercise nor assigned any work. After much prodding the prison superintendent consented to a brief exercise drill.

General Jaap van Deventer (left), Jan Smuts (middle) and Salmon Gerhardus (right) in the northern Cape in 1902 during the Second Boer War, also known as the South African War

Albert Cartwright, the editor of the *Transvaal Leader* and a supporter of the Indian cause, negotiated a settlement with the Boer leader, General Jan Christiaan Smuts. Under the proposed plan, registration for the Indians would become voluntary and—provided a majority of Indians completed the registration process—the British would repeal the Black Act. Gandhi suggested changes to strengthen and clarify the way in which the repeal would take place. He was taken out of jail and brought to Pretoria to meet with General Smuts. After Smuts and Gandhi agreed to the compromise, Gandhi was officially released from prison. Gandhi had no money and General Smuts had to pay for his railway fare back to Johannesburg.

The following evening Gandhi called a meeting in Johannesburg and spoke to the more than one thousand Indians who had gathered. Gandhi had found his voice. At the end of his lengthy and persuasive speech the assembled group voted to accept the settlement. Only a handful voted against it.

Gandhi wanted to set an example by being among the first to apply—voluntarily—for his registration certificate. On February 10, 1908, as he headed out to the Registrar's office, he was greeted by Mir

Alam, an angry former client, who opposed the settlement. Mir Alam and his companions attacked Gandhi and knocked him unconscious. Gandhi's cheek and lip were badly cut; still, no sooner had he recovered than he insisted on being the first to register. He wanted everyone else to follow suit and issued a statement saying, "No cowardly fear therefore should deter the vast majority of sober-minded Indians from doing their duty."

Although many Indians applied for registration certificates, by August 1908 it became clear that General Smuts would not repeal the Black Act. Writing in the *Indian Opinion*, Gandhi warned his readers that the voluntary registration had failed and that they would need to start a new satyagraha campaign. Gandhi asked the Indians to burn their registration certificates and be prepared to go to jail.

On August 16, the Satyagraha Committee planned an enormous bonfire. The flames lit up the night sky as 2,000 certificates were set on fire. Gandhi told the assembled crowd, "By burning the certificates we only declare our solemn resolution never to submit to the Black Act."

Many satyagrahis were arrested for traveling into the Transvaal without a certificate. Since it was necessary to show a registration certificate in order to obtain a trading license, those satyagrahis who stayed within the Transvaal but applied for trading licenses were also arrested and imprisoned. Going to jail was a sacrifice they were more than willing to make.

On October 15, 1908, Gandhi was arrested and put in solitary confinement. His diet was strictly limited, as were opportunities for exercise. For the next several months Gandhi stayed in jail, was released, and then re-arrested. On each occasion Gandhi criticized the government for their harsh treatment of Indians—each arrest helped serve the satyagraha cause.

Gandhi had little time to read outside prison, but did find time while he was in jail. He came across Henry David Thoreau's essay "On Civil Disobedience" in the prison library. Here Thoreau calls on men to follow their own conscience and to disobey the government

An 1854 drawing of Henry David Thoreau
by Samuel Worcester Rouse

if need be. Gandhi read the essay with great interest and found he had much in common with the American author. Thoreau had chosen to live a simple life to stand up for his principles—refusing to pay taxes to protest the government's role in the Mexican-American War and slavery. Thoreau, like Gandhi, had discovered "how deep [were] the ruts of tradition and conformity." Both men sought that which was less tangible than wealth. "Rather than love, than money, than fame . . . give me truth," Thoreau wrote. This became one of Gandhi's guiding principles. For a while Gandhi even used the term "civil disobedience" to explain satyagraha to English speakers. However, he later veered away from the word "disobedience," using the term "civil resistance" instead.

In prison Gandhi was allowed to write one letter per month. On March 25, 1909, he wrote to his son Manilal, "I have often felt that you required greater personal guidance than I have been able to give you. I know too that you have sometimes felt that your education was being neglected. . . . [E]ducation does not mean a knowledge of letters but it means character building. It means a knowledge of duty . . . Remember please that henceforth our lot is poverty. The more I think of it the more I feel it is more blessed to be poor than to be rich." Now that Gandhi was in prison he had ample time to instruct his son. The letter includes advice to study gardening, mathematics, Sanskrit, and music. He adds, "Never get agitated and think you have too much to do and then worry over what to do first."

Government officials in the Transvaal were beginning to realize that imprisonment was not effective. They chose a more cruel punishment—deportation. Satyagraha now carried a greater risk. In July 1909, Gandhi traveled to London once again to plead the Indian cause. In meetings with British leaders, journalists, and members of Parliament, he asked for the repeal of the Black Act and the lifting of restrictions on immigration.

Gandhi, as always, showed respect for those who disagreed with him and easily engaged them in the issues. But after four months he was unable to persuade the British to change their laws. On the voyage back to South Africa he wrote *Hind Swaraj (Indian Home Rule)*, a pamphlet calling for a movement away from a centralized government that would make self-rule possible. Here Gandhi also discusses satyagraha and the need to strengthen the power of individual communities. In years to come Gandhi would re-affirm his devotion to the philosophy behind *Hind Swaraj*.

Back in South Africa, Gandhi devised a plan to establish a settlement where satyagrahis could live together and share both chores and expenses. His friend, Hermann Kallenbach, a successful and wealthy architect, bought a large farm twenty-one miles from Johannesburg. Hundreds of fruit trees—orange, apricot and plum—grew on the land. Sixty men, women, and children from different regions of India and diverse faiths settled on the property—building houses, erecting a school and a carpentry workshop. The residents attended to all the chores themselves—they cooked, cleaned, and cared for the land. They used one kitchen and took their meals together. A typical meal included a mixture of rice, dhal (a dish made of dried beans and lentils), and vegetables. Standards for cleanliness were high—rubbish was buried or used as manure.

The residents were encouraged to be self-reliant—Kallenbach even taught them to make their own sandals. If they wanted to go to Johannesburg, Gandhi insisted they walk. They were to bring food with them so there would be no need to spend money in the city. Gandhi himself often walked back and forth in one day—leaving at 2 a.m. and returning in the evening.

Albert West (top left), Hermann Kallenbach (front left),
and Mohandas Gandhi at Tolstoy Farm in South Africa

Gandhi called the community the Tolstoy Farm after the writer he so much admired. Throughout the year he corresponded with Tolstoy about his new project. Tolstoy wrote Gandhi about his philosophy on nonresistance and the problems the world faced, such as "the growth of crime, freedom from toil, the increasingly absurd luxury of the rich and increased misery of the poor, the fearfully rising number of suicides." He shared his faith that they would be resolved "in such a manner that the law of love will be recognized and all reliance on force abandoned." After Tolstoy died on November 20, 1910, Gandhi wrote in the *Indian Opinion* that he would endeavor to follow Tolstoy's teaching.

Kallenbach and Gandhi organized a school for the children. Gandhi found teaching one of his more challenging tasks. Students in the one-room school ranged in age from seven to twenty and spoke several different languages—it was hard to keep them all engaged at the same time. Students did their chores in the morning so they were often exhausted by the time they came to class in the afternoon.

Every evening the residents offered prayers in three languages—Gujarati, Hindi, and English. They sang hymns and read from the Qur'an, the sacred book of Muslims, and the *Ramayana*, an ancient text sacred to Hindus. By 9 p.m. they were ready to retire. They had to wake early to begin their chores. Gandhi watched over the farm and cared for those who were sick. No one was given medication—Gandhi was a strong proponent of diet and home remedies.

In 1912 Gandhi invited his friend and mentor Gopal Krishna Gokhale to visit. One of India's most highly respected political leaders, Gokhale arrived in South Africa and met with both Indians and whites, as well as government officials. He spoke eloquently on equal rights for Indians—many whites found him persuasive. Before returning to India, Gokhale assured Gandhi that not only would the Black Act be repealed and the immigration laws reformed, but that the £3 tax, the tax indentured servants had to pay once they had completed their years of servitude, would be removed. Gokhale was so confident that conditions in South Africa would improve that he urged Gandhi to return to India—his leadership would be needed there. Gandhi agreed.

General Smuts, however, refused to consider the abolition of the £3 tax. Indentured servants now had cause to join the satyagraha movement. In addition Indians were made to endure yet another form of discrimination—their marriages were no longer to be considered valid or legal. In India no registration for a marriage was necessary—the religious ceremony sufficed. The government in South Africa, however, would not recognize these marriages because they were not registered. Indian wives would now be considered concubines and their rights denied. Gandhi delayed his departure to India so that he could address these issues and help put reforms in place.

Several satyagrahis entered the Transvaal without permits. Kasturbai also chose to participate—she and the others were arrested. On September 23, 1913, they received a sentence of three months' imprisonment with hard labor. Other satyagrahi volunteers chose a different form of protest: They went on strike—they too were arrested and put in jail. They were fed poorly and some became sick.

Laborers at the mines in Newcastle, a town in Natal, were inspired to go on strike. Hundreds joined the movement. Soon the strikers numbered more than 2,000. Gandhi wanted them to take their protest to the Transvaal in protest. The railway fare was costly so they decided to go by foot and to march together.

Before the march got underway Gandhi received an invitation to speak with the mine owners in Durban. They urged him to put an end to the strike. Gandhi explained that he would end the strike if and when the government repealed the £3 tax. When the mine owners refused, Gandhi set in motion his plans for the thirty-six mile march. There was to be no turning back.

Gandhi prepared the miners for the long trek to be led by members of the Phoenix settlement. He asked them to carry as little as possible for the two-day journey—they would need to survive on a daily ration of a pound and a half of bread and an ounce of sugar. If Gandhi was arrested they must continue the march.

On October 28, 1913, the miners set out for Charlestown on the border of Natal and the Transvaal. Gandhi had arrived before them and prepared a dish of rice, dhal, and vegetables. When the marchers arrived he and his helpers greeted them and served them a warm meal. Gandhi contacted General Smuts, this time by phone, and said he would stop the march if the £3 tax were abolished. If not, they would enter the Transvaal. "I will not break the law merely for the sake of breaking it but I am driven to it by inexorable necessity." General Smuts's reply was direct and curt: he refused to abolish the tax.

The group, now composed of 2,037 men, 127 women and 57 children, crossed the border into the Transvaal. They had been warned that the whites might shoot, but there was no gunfire. The marchers went on their way and stopped at night to rest. While they slept Gandhi was arrested and taken by train to Volksrust. He had to appear in court but was released on bail. He immediately rejoined the march. Within four days he was arrested and released on three occasions. But his followers never became discouraged. The march continued.

Gandhi was arrested again on November 11, 1913, for inducing laborers to leave Natal. This time he received a sentence of nine months imprisonment with hard labor. He was kept in a cell with little ventilation and isolated from other Indians. The jail's doctors made sure Gandhi's limited diet—bananas, tomatoes, nuts, limes and olive oil—was made available to him. Other leaders of the march, Hermann Kallenbach and Henry S. L. Polak, were also imprisoned.

Meanwhile, laborers in other parts of Natal went on strike. Mounted military police responded by forcing the strikers to return to work—or by opening fire if they refused. Thousands of persons went to jail. Gandhi knew the government could ill afford to keep them imprisoned. In December 1913, the British Viceroy of India, Lord Hardinge, made a speech in which he strongly criticized the British government—speaking out against the South African legislation and in defense of satyagraha. "General Smuts too saw that there had been injustice which called for remedy, but he was in the same predicament as a snake which has taken a rat in its mouth but can neither gulp it down nor cast

Stopped at Border Volksrust.

A photo of the Great March to the Transvaal in 1913

it out," Gandhi wrote later in an account of what became known as the "Great March."

General Smuts recognized the wrongs and hardships the Indians had endured, but he also felt pressure from white South Africans not to abolish the tax. He set up a commission to make recommendations to the state. However, no Indian representatives were on the commission.

After serving six weeks in prison, Gandhi, Kallenbach and Polak were released. As soon as Gandhi heard of Smuts' commission he protested the lack of Indian representation. He announced that satyagrahis should again ready themselves for jail and start a new march if need be. He traveled to Pretoria to meet with General Smuts and to explain his actions. Charles Freer Andrews, a Christian missionary who became a close friend of Gandhi, assisted him in his mission.

General Smuts refused to allow Indian representation—but he conceded on a major issue, agreeing—for the first time—to support the abolition of the tax. However, charges against soldiers who had harmed Indian laborers would have to be dropped. Gandhi believed satyagrahis had to suffer in order to accomplish their goals. He was willing to drop the charges and he convinced others to do the same. "A Satyagrahi fights only for essentials. The essential thing was that the obnoxious laws should be repealed or suitably amended, and when this was fairly within his grasp, he need not bother himself with other things," he explained.

Gandhi and Charles Andrews continued to work out the details with General Smuts and convinced the Indians to suspend satyagraha even though they had little reason to trust Smuts. After much deliberation the commission issued its report advocating reforms—and this time, Smuts proved trustworthy. The Indian Relief Bill became law in July 1914. Indian marriages were now considered legal and valid. The tax on indentured laborers who had finished their service and did not return to India was abolished. Indians, however, did not receive full rights to travel between provinces or to own land.

Gandhi and General Smuts had been at odds for more than seven years, yet General Smuts had the utmost respect for Gandhi and years later would wear with pride the pair of sandals Gandhi had made for him.

Gandhi believed that satyagrahis would continue to influence the government to make further changes by influencing and educating public opinion. For now the battle was over and the satyagrahis had won. Gandhi had shown that "Satyagraha is a priceless and matchless weapon, and that those who wield it are strangers to disappointment or defeat."

CHAPTER SIX

Swaraj in India

Before returning to India, Gandhi decided to take Kasturbai to Great Britain. They arrived on August 6, 1914, two days after the British government declared war on Germany. World War I had begun. Millions would die before it ended.

Once again Gandhi volunteered for ambulance work. Many of his friends questioned his willingness to serve in the war given his strong belief in ahimsa (nonviolence). Gandhi agreed that "participation in war could never be consistent with ahimsa," but countered that it was difficult to choose between ahimsa and duty. His pacifist friends remained skeptical, yet Gandhi charted his own course.

Gandhi's service in the ambulance corps turned out to be both problematic and short-lived. The British commanding officer had trouble relinquishing any authority to Gandhi. The Indian volunteers, on the other hand, expected to take orders from Gandhi, not the commanding officer. Then Gandhi began to suffer from pleurisy, an inflammation of the lungs, and became bedridden. His doctor advised him to return to India.

Gandhi with his wife
Kasturbai the year
before their departure
for England

In December 1914, Gandhi and his wife left England for India.
During the voyage he was careful about his diet, eating mostly nuts and
dried fruit, and his health gradually improved.

Gandhi's work in South Africa had made him famous in his home-
land. When he and Kasturbai arrived in Bombay Gandhi attended parties in his honor, including a grand reception at a palace and a more
modest function hosted by the Gujaratis. The speeches were given in
English but Gandhi had come to favor the use of native languages and
replied to the speeches in Gujarati. His choice of language was a polite
form of protest, the first of many he would make in India.

Old friends welcomed him home. The poet Rabindranath Tagore, who had won the Nobel Prize for Literature in 1913, called him
"Mahatma," meaning "The Great Soul." Gokhale, a leader in the independence movement, greeted him warmly.

At Gokhale's suggestion, Gandhi spent a year traveling throughout India, learning as much as he could about the country he had been away for more than twenty years. Wherever he went, he met and talked with people from all castes and walks of life, Hindu as well as Muslim. He adopted the traditional Hindu hairstyle, called a *shikha*, a tuft of hair on the crown of his head. He simplified his wardrobe and wore only a loincloth.

Gokhale now headed the Indian National Congress, a group first established in 1885 to give Indians a greater role in their own government. Its members met to discuss Indian grievances and to campaign for political rights.

But long before the establishment of the Indian National Congress, there had been many attempts by peasants, tribal communities, and princely states to eliminate colonial rule in India. British Crown rule began in 1858, yet prior to Crown rule India had been controlled by the East India Company, which was comprised of British traders. In 1600, Elizabeth, then the monarch of the United Kingdom, had given the large group of merchants monopoly privileges on all trade with the East Indies. The company's first ships landed at the port of Surat in India in 1608.

Over time, the East India Company evolved into a ruling enterprise, but not without resistance from the Indian people. Between 1763 and 1856, armed revolts broke out practically every year. However, the British, with their superior guns and communication networks, always managed to brutally suppress the uprisings.

The East Indian Company dissolved in 1858, and the British Raj took over. But before the Raj could formalize its control, Indians fought back. India's First War of Independence—also termed the Sepoy Riots, the Sepoy Mutiny, the Great Rebellion, and the Indian Rebellion— lasted nearly two years, from 1857 to 1858.

So while the establishment of the Indian National Congress marked a key turning point in formalized opposition to the Raj, nationalist feelings had long simmered in India.

Great Britain in India

Britain had both colonies and dependencies when it began its rule in India in 1858. Canada and Australia, for example, were colonies, meaning the countries were nominally governed by Britain and exercised self-rule in most matters except their relations to foreign powers. India, on the other hand, was primarily a dependency. As a dependency, it was ruled by Great Britain and granted no self-government or representation, meaning it had no political freedom.

The British built tens of thousands of miles of railway, as well as canals and irrigation systems in India. They established good postal and telegraph systems, an English education system, with many schools and colleges, hospitals, courts of law patterned after the English system, and they created conditions for growth of industry that brought India in line with the world economy. However, these developments mostly benefited the English and not Indians, who were growing poorer under British rule. In 1850, the average daily income of the people of India was estimated at four cents a person. In 1882, it was down to three cents, and by 1900 it had fallen to less than two cents a person. Worse, British practices made India more prone to devastating famines: millions perished.

India was a rich country when the British first arrived. It manufactured cotton, silk, pottery, and jewelry, among other goods, and these were prized all over the world. But those industries began to die out after the British passed successive excise laws and tariffs to ruin India's manufacturers. With India's manufacturers out of the way, the British secured India's market for its own manufacturers. The millions of people who had depended on those Indian manufacturers for employment were then forced back on the land, to scrape out a living alongside farmers who were barely making it. And to make matters worse, the British began imposing excessively high taxes on the Indian people, who were already largely impoverished. In 1905, for example, the annual average income per person in India was about six dollars, and the annual tax per person was about two dollars.

Other factors leading to the impoverishment of Indians under British rule included the high cost of running the government of India—nearly all the high officials were British and not Indians—and the enormous expense of maintaining the military. The military expense was so high that Sir Henry Campbell-Bannerman, prime minister of the United Kingdom from 1905 to 1908, acknowledged that it was a burden: "Justice demands that England should pay a portion of the cost of the great Indian Army maintained in India for Imperial rather than Indian purposes. . . . famine-stricken India is being bled for the maintenance of England's worldwide empire," he said.

As the years under British rule progressed, and the suffering of Indians deepened, the nationalist movement gained momentum. Indian writer, Jabez T. Sutherland, asked the question "Why is England in India at all?" In a 1908 article he wrote:

> Perhaps the greatest of all the causes of the impoverishment of the Indian people is the steady and enormous drain of wealth from India to England. . . . In the form of salaries spent in England, pensions sent to England, interest drawn in England on investments made in India, business profits made in India and sent to England, and various kinds of exploitation carried on in India for England's benefit, a vast stream of wealth is constantly pouring into England from India.

Though the independence movement had existed ever since the Raj had begun in 1858, at first it had attracted only a small following. But the movement gained strength during World War I. After Gokhale's death in 1915, Gandhi became the new leader of the Congress. He helped institute constitutional reforms and worked to bring together people from different religions to work towards common goals. At first his goal was not to cut all ties to Britain, but for India to become a self-governing part of the British Empire.

As Gandhi became more involved in the independence movement he had to give up his law practice so he could devote himself full-time to his cause. He established an ashram, a place where he and his family could live together with members of a community who shared his values. He chose a place called Sabamarti, outside Ahmedabad, the capital of Gujarat and a center of handloom weaving. Twenty Indians from different parts of the country as well as five Tamil youth from South Africa shared their housing, their food, and their daily lives. They named the ashram Satyagraha and vowed to live according to its principles. Their huts were situated in a grove of trees—Gandhi occupied a room with one window—outside was a small terrace where he slept. Possessions were considered unimportant.

A full scale replica of Gandhi's room in the Sabarmati Ashram at Ahmedabad in Gujarat, India, on display at the National Gandhi Museum in New Delhi, India

As Gandhi continued his work on the ashram he became more revered—and more loved. People came to the ashram to learn about satyagraha. They attended Gandhi's daily prayer meetings and learned to appreciate the communal lifestyle. When visitors saw that members of the ashram had taken in a family of "untouchables" (the poorest of the castes) their attitudes towards this group began to change and gradually their fears subsided. Many left transformed—they would become Gandhi's followers and teach others about satyagraha.

In February 1917, a resolution to stop the emigration of indentured servants from India was introduced in the Congress. Gandhi resolved to help by encouraging "an all-India agitation." The viceroy, Lord Chelmsford, met with Gandhi and appeared supportive of the resolution, but refused to offer a timetable for instituting the reform. Gandhi toured the country by third-class train, traveling from Calcutta in the east to Lahore in the northwest. Everywhere he went he stressed the importance of stopping indentured emigration. Within six months the British government agreed to put the resolution into effect. Gandhi had shown that he could effect change by mounting a public awareness campaign.

The plight of indigo workers in Champaran, a region bordering Nepal, also caught Gandhi's attention. Rajkumar Shukla, a farmer from Champaran, met Gandhi at a meeting of the Congress and persuaded him to visit the indigo plantations in Champaran to learn about the farmers' many hardships. Indigo had been widely used as a dye for textiles. The British landlords had required that their tenant farmers plant 15 percent of their land with indigo and donate the indigo harvest to the landlords in lieu of rent. After a synthetic dye was developed the demand for indigo decreased. The landlords no longer demanded the tenants produce indigo; now they demanded that the tenants pay unreasonably high fees they could ill afford.

Gandhi traveled north to the foot of the Himalayas to begin his investigation. The police suspected this would only lead to trouble and ordered him to leave the area. Gandhi refused, received a summons, and was arrested.

Showing no signs of anger, Gandhi spoke calmly and insisted his acts of civil disobedience were not personal attacks. Upon arriving in court he explained that he had come to help the farmers who were unfairly treated by their landlords. "As a law-abiding citizen my first instinct would be, as it was, to obey the order served upon me. But I could not do so without doing violence to my sense of duty to those for whom I have come." The only "safe and honorable course" for him would be "to submit without protest to the penalty of disobedience." Gandhi sent telegrams to the viceroy and leaders of Congress and gave a clear explanation of his actions. The case against him was withdrawn.

Gandhi's defiance of the law and his willingness to pay the consequences drew attention to the farmers' grievances. Gandhi continued his inquiry and tried not to "irritate" the planters, "but to win them over by gentleness." Gandhi and his co-workers collected 10,000 depositions from farmers—more than sufficient evidence of their mistreatment. The British landlords eventually admitted defeat and agreed to repay a portion of the fees they had collected.

Gandhi devoted an entire year to the Champaran campaign. During this time he was struck by the extreme poverty in the region—the unsanitary conditions, the absence of health workers, the need for education. Children spent their days in the fields—there were no schools. Now that the landlords were no longer charging their tenants high fees, Gandhi wanted to bring about other changes as well. He recruited volunteer teachers (including his son Devdas and his assistant Mahadev Desai). He opened primary schools in six villages. Gandhi's friend, Dr. Narendra Dev, offered his medical services for six months and trained volunteers to dispense three medicines—castor oil, quinine, and sulfur—with which almost all medical problems could be treated. Kasturbai came to Champaran to provide education in sanitation. Great efforts were made to clean the wells and remove waste from courtyards, roads, and lanes.

Once the situation at Champaran improved, Gandhi, never one to rest, turned his attention to the plight of textile laborers in Ahmedabad. Their wages were low, their hours long, and the work was demanding. Gandhi suggested the mill-owners refer the dispute to arbitration, but they refused. Gandhi advised the laborers to strike. He insisted they never resort to violence or molest strikebreakers, and he urged them to "remain firm, no matter how long the strike continued, and to earn bread, during the strike, by any other honest labor." Thousands went on strike. Every day Gandhi met with them under the shade of a tree to remind them of their pledge.

But, after two weeks, the strikers began to waver; many of them no longer attended the daily meeting. They started to show their anger towards the strike-breakers—Gandhi thought a riot might break out. He called the mill-workers together and began to speak: "Unless the strikers rally and continue the strike till a settlement is reached . . . I will not touch any food." Gandhi had not previously mentioned the possibility of fasting. The words simply came out of his mouth. The laborers were "thunderstruck" by his offer—they were touched by his selflessness and wanted to join him in his fast.

Gandhi made it clear that he fasted not in personal opposition to the mill-owners—he held the mill-owner and leader of the opposition, Sheth Ambalal, and his wife in high regard. The fast was to show his support for the strike and to re-energize the mill-workers. Gandhi insisted the struggle be peaceful—and civil. This civility was the most difficult part of satyagraha. Gandhi explained that this did not mean "the outward gentleness of speech," but "an inborn gentleness and desire to do the opponent good." His actions had the desired effect: a positive feeling resulted and, after a twenty-one-day strike and Gandhi's three-day fast, a settlement was reached.

Meanwhile, Europe was being transformed as the world war waged on. Empires unraveled and revolutions born. During the Russian Revolution of 1917, the Tsar had been deposed and the Bolsheviks, a part of the Communist Party, seized power. In 1918, the Central Powers

(Austria-Hungary, Germany, Bulgaria, and the Ottoman Empire) were defeated.

The war had exhausted Europe. The British had been on the winning side but were so weakened that the future of their empire could no longer be assured. The burgeoning struggle for independence in India, especially in the Punjab and Bengal, alarmed them. British leaders suspected both the Germans and the Bolsheviks were responsible for many of the disturbances and much of the tension. The British appointed Justice Sidney Rowlatt to head a committee to study the role of the Germans and Bolsheviks in undermining the British government in India. The Rowlatt Committee found there was little threat from the Bolsheviks, but believed during the war the Germans had offered their support to the Indian independence movement and may have encouraged acts of terrorism—using acts of violence to instill fear for political purposes. The legislation they recommended to combat this alarmed Gandhi. What would become known as the "Rowlatt bills" gave the British government the power to imprison anyone in India they suspected of terrorism without a trial.

Justice Sidney Rowlatt

Gandhi wanted the people to take a satyagraha pledge of civil, nonviolent resistance to oppose these measures. He also appealed in public and private letters to the viceroy—but to no avail. On March 18, 1919, the bills were passed and martial law, the establishment of military rule, was established.

That night Gandhi pondered what to do. As if he was "in that twilight condition between sleep and consciousness" he thought of calling on the country to observe a hartal—or strike. His friends warmed to the suggestion: "Let all the people of India, therefore, suspend their business on that day and observe the day as one of fasting and prayer," Gandhi declared. Hindus and Muslims were united in the decision to strike and many would come together to march in procession on the first day. The date was set for March 30, 1919, and then changed to April 6. Those in Delhi did not learn of the change in date. Their hartal was held on March 30, but they were not properly prepared and violence erupted. The police opened fire and riots broke out—leaving the city in a state of turmoil. The hartal in Bombay on April 6, however, was successful—workers risked arrest and imprisonment to participate in the strike but did not resort to violence. They handed out thousands of copies of Gandhi's *Hind Swaraj*—the distribution of which the government had prohibited.

News of the shooting and rioting in Delhi distressed Gandhi. After the April 6 hartal in Bombay, he boarded a train for Delhi, planning to investigate the repercussions of the March 30 strike. Shortly before reaching Palwal (thirty-seven miles from Delhi), Gandhi received a notice that he would be prohibited from entering the region because it would cause a disturbance. Gandhi refused to turn around and explained that he was going to Delhi not to cause trouble but to put an end to the violence. Still the police arrested him. Gandhi sent word to Delhi that the people should maintain "perfect peace" no matter what punishment he was given. In so doing they would show that satyagraha was winning.

Gandhi was taken to Bombay and eventually released. The people gathered to form a joyful procession. The mounted police, fearing a riot, charged on the crowd to disperse it. People were trampled and crushed. Gandhi later paid a visit to the commissioner to protest the actions of the police and explain the goals of satyagraha. The commissioner remained unmoved.

Violence broke out in other parts of India. Gandhi traveled to Ahmedabad where he discovered that the mill-workers had rioted and a sergeant had been killed. Gandhi knew satyagraha could only succeed if the people were nonviolent. In Ahmedabad innocent people were killed, shops and homes looted, buildings burned. Gandhi went on to other cities in Gujarat—there too the people had not followed the principle of ahimsa. They had embraced neither universal love nor civil resistance, but committed one act of violence after another.

Gandhi decided to suspend his campaign. He had misjudged the people's readiness to participate in civil disobedience. He considered his error so great that it was of Himalayan proportion. He called it the "Himalayan miscalculation." A satyagrahi must act nonviolently and be willing to pay the penalty for disobedience—the people had not shown the strength of character necessary to become a satyagrahi.

Throughout the Punjab, government buildings and railway stations were burned. Telegraph posts were destroyed, and rioting increased. As tension mounted in Amritsar, a city in the Punjab, General Reginald Dyer banned public meetings and processions. Nevertheless, thousands of people gathered on April 13, 1919, at the Jallianwalla Bagh, an open area near the Golden Temple, a holy place in Amritsar. General Dyer led ninety government soldiers to the Jallianwalla Bagh. Fifty soldiers were armed with guns; the remainder carried knives. Without giving a warning to the crowd General Dyer ordered his soldiers to open fire: 1,650 rounds were shot and at least 379 people were killed. (Some estimate that the number was much higher.) More than 1,100 were injured.

General Dyer showed no remorse. In the midst of the rioting a missionary schoolteacher, Miss Sherwood, had been viciously attacked. A few days later General Dyer issued the crawling order—all those who passed by the street where the attack occurred would have to do so on their hands and knees.

A 1919 photograph of a street in Punjab, India,
during the martial law regime

When Gandhi heard of the Amritsar massacre he asked to enter the Punjab so he could lead an investigation. He was granted permission—the Indians who greeted him were "delirious with joy." His report showed "to what lengths the British government is capable of going, and what inhumanities and barbarities it is capable of perpetrating in order to maintain its power." General Dyer later admitted that he could have dispersed the crowd without firing—but he had wanted to punish them. The British eventually asked him to resign from the army, but General Dyer suffered no other consequences.

An artist's impression of the massacre at Amritsar, India

Gandhi decided people needed to be educated in satyagraha before they could use the method effectively. He took on the writing and editing of two publications that he would use to teach the principles of satyagraha. One was *Young India*, an English-language journal, and the other was *Navajivan*, written in Gujarati. Gandhi set up his own printing press in Ahmedabad and published the two journals without interference from business or government interests. Both were distributed widely.

In November 1919, Gandhi was invited to a Muslim conference in Delhi, also attended by Hindus. India's relationship to Britain was discussed.

Gandhi expressed his view that the only effective "true resistance" to the British government would be "to cease to cooperate with it." If the government imposed unfavorable terms "it is an inalienable right of the people thus to withhold cooperation." It was here that Gandhi introduced for the first time the term "non-cooperation." Non-cooperation was not passive, but "intensely active." It must be "non-violent and, therefore, neither punitive nor vindictive nor based on malice, ill-will or hatred."

Gandhi also stressed that Indians needed to rely less on British imports—he believed in the importance of celebrating work that was done by hand. Members at the ashram wanted to use only cloth made from Indian yarn and woven on handlooms—not mill-woven cloth. They started to spin their own yarn and made a coarse cloth called khaddar. Gandhi used this for his dhoti—the traditional male clothing that wraps around the waist and legs. He believed that the production of khaddar could create jobs for the unemployed and help feed the hungry.

In 1920, Gandhi, now president of the All-India Home Rule League, the political party that supported Indian independence, was asked to rewrite the constitution for Congress. He proposed that the goal of Congress was to attain—peacefully and legitimately—swaraj (self-governance or home-rule). India could remain part of the British Empire if Indians would be allowed to govern themselves; if not, they would have to make a clean break.

Gandhi's agenda included resolutions to support Hindu-Muslim unity and rid the country of the "curse of untouchability." "It is a sin to believe anyone else is inferior or superior to ourselves. We are all equal . . . . What crimes for which we condemn the [British] Government as satanic, have not we been guilty of toward our untouchable brethren? . . . It is idle to talk of *Swaraj* so long as we do not protect the weak and the helpless or so long as it is possible for a single *Swarajist* to injure the feelings of any individual."

Gandhi insisted swaraj could not be achieved by his efforts alone or those of Hindus. They would need to be joined by Muslims, Parsis, Christians, Sikhs, Jews, all other Indians, and the English.

Traveling throughout the country, Gandhi spread the message of noncooperation and swaraj. If the people practiced noncooperation and were at the same time nonviolent, they would achieve swaraj. Indians were encouraged not to pay taxes, to give up alcohol, to renounce British titles, and to return their medals. Gandhi returned his as an example. He asked Indians to boycott British schools, not take government jobs, and give up British exports, including all clothing not made in India. Foreign clothing was burned. Wherever Gandhi went he urged the people to learn to spin and weave.

On February 2, 1922, the residents in Chauri Chaura, a small town in the north of India, organized a demonstration. They received threats from the police and responded by setting fire to the city hall where the police were stationed. Twenty-two policemen were killed, some of them hacked to death.

The tragic violence was deeply disturbing to Gandhi. He wanted India to achieve her independence—but not through bloodshed. Violent tactics were unacceptable. He had planned a mass nonviolent resistance movement to take place across the country, but now he would suspend it. He would wait until the people were ready to resist nonviolently. He would also fast for five days—an act that he hoped would underscore his strongly held belief that change must occur peacefully.

British officials in London and India wanted the viceroy, Lord Reading, to arrest Gandhi for sedition—rebellion against the government—but Lord Reading was reluctant. He had met Gandhi and admired his frank and courteous demeanor as well as his deep convictions. However, Lord Reading eventually gave in to the pressure. On March 10, 1922, a police officer arrested Gandhi at the ashram at Sabamarti. He submitted without complaint and was taken to the jail. The following morning Kasturbai brought him clothes, goat's milk, and grapes. Gandhi's arrest and imprisonment would shine a spotlight on their cause—Kasturbai, like her husband, took solace in that.

Gandhi was charged with writing three seditious articles in *Young India* in which he had advocated the use of noncooperation to overthrow the government. "How can there be any compromise whilst the British lion continues to shake his gory claws in our faces?" he asked. Gandhi had discovered in South Africa that as an Indian he had no rights. He had fought "to gain a status of full equality in the Empire." But that was not to be. Now he was back in his native country. "The British connection had made India more helpless than she ever was before." He stated that he had "no personal ill-will against any administrator" nor towards the King's person. "In my opinion, non-cooperation with evil is as much a duty as is cooperation with good."

Gandhi pleaded guilty and asked to receive the highest penalty. He was sentenced to six years' imprisonment.

CHAPTER SEVEN

"Love Never Claims"

On January 12, 1924, Gandhi suddenly became ill with appendicitis and had to be rushed from the Sabamarti prison to the hospital in Poona. A British surgeon would have to perform the operation—there was no time to call an Indian doctor. Gandhi and the British doctors worried that a failed medical procedure would alarm people all across India and set in motion a nationwide insurrection. Gandhi would not let the operation proceed until he had prepared a public statement explaining that he had agreed to the operation and that the physicians had treated him well. There must be no anti-government agitation whatever the outcome of the operation.

As soon as Gandhi signed the document the anesthetic was administered. The operating conditions were less than ideal: A thunderstorm put out the electricity so a flashlight was used. After that stopped working a hurricane lamp was found. Gandhi's recovery was slow and the government decided it was best to release him from prison.

After twenty-two months in jail, Gandhi found little had changed. No advances had been made to bring about unity between the Hindus and Muslims. Writing for *Young India*, Gandhi called for all people to adopt nonviolence as their creed: "Make our hearts as broad as the ocean. That is the teaching of the Koran and of the Gita . . . Love never claims, it ever gives. Love ever suffers, never resents, never revenges itself. . . . Non-violence is the summit of bravery," he assured his readers.

On September 18, 1924, when Gandhi was fifty-five years old and still suffering from the aftermath of the operation, he planned a twenty-one day fast. He was willing to risk his life for the cause he held dear—Hindu-Muslim friendship. Two Muslim doctors and his missionary friend Charles Freer Andrews looked after him. Gandhi hoped that his fast would prove more persuasive than his words—that it would bring the two communities together. On the 21st day, Bapu, as his friends and family affectionately called him, prepared to break the fast. He asked all those who were caring for him to be willing to sacrifice their lives for the cause of friendship. Verses from the Qur'an and the Upanishads, the sacred Hindu scriptures, were read—and a Christian hymn, "When I Survey the Wondrous Cross," was sung.

For the next few years Gandhi became increasingly committed to promoting hand-spinning and hand-weaving. He identified with the laboring classes and continued to encourage everyone to wear khaddar, homespun cloth. During meetings members of Congress talked while spinning on collapsible spinning wheels. "For me, the spinning wheel is not only a symbol of simplicity and economic freedom, but it is also a symbol of peace," Gandhi wrote in *Young India*. Soon everyone who wanted an independent India was wearing khaddar. The spinning wheel was a powerful tool—it brought people together, made them self-reliant and would help them achieve independence.

The ashram was still home to Gandhi—a place where he could lead a simple life. "I own no property and yet I feel that I am perhaps the richest man in the world." Here he strengthened his ties to the community. Many who admired him from afar came to visit—and some stayed. Madeleine Slade, daughter of a British admiral, was one who remained. She had heard of Gandhi from Romain Rolland, a French author and pacifist who greatly admired him. She was intrigued by his story and wanted not only to meet him, but to become part of his life. Before traveling to India, she read Hindu scriptures and all of Gandhi's writings. She learned the rules of the ashram and worked in the hay-

Gandhi repairs his charkha spinning wheel
with the assistance of Madeleine Slade

fields to become fit. She studied Urdu, a language spoken in parts of India, and she learned to spin. At the age of thirty-three, she came to Sabamarti, adopted Indian dress and a vegetarian diet, shaved her head, and took on daily chores.

"You shall be my daughter," Gandhi told her. Madeleine and Gandhi formed a close friendship, talking regularly and corresponding when they were apart. She found him "full of love and gentleness," but recognized that "in his fight with evil he was relentless."

Over the years, Gandhi's views on women had changed. He no longer believed that women needed to be completely subservient to men. Now he campaigned to raise their status. He opposed child marriages and wanted women to be taught to think independently.

In 1925 Gandhi traveled throughout India by train and by foot. Everywhere he went crowds of people greeted him, calling him "Mahatma." He gave speeches and stressed not only swaraj (home rule), but also harmony. "My attitude towards the English is one of utter friendliness and respect. I claim to be their friend, because it is contrary to my nature to distrust a single human being." He recognized their bravery and their spirit of sacrifice. "By a long course of prayerful discipline I have ceased for over forty years to hate anybody. I know this is a big claim. But I can and do hate evil wherever it exists. I hate the system of Government the British people have set up in India." He abhorred "the ruthless exploitation of India" by the British as well as "the hideous system of untouchability for which millions of Hindus have made themselves responsible"—but he hated neither the British nor the Hindus. He collected money for the untouchables and also accepted jewelry which he sold, giving the proceeds to the poor.

Gandhi's journeys left him exhausted. In August 1925, he wrote, "It has often occurred to me that a seeker after truth has to be silent. . . . We do not know very often what we say. If we want to listen to the still small voice that is always speaking within us, it will not be heard if we continually speak." A few months later, he made the decision to rest for one year—and to learn from silence. On Mondays he would not talk at all. The plan worked—he still talked to people, but never on a Monday, and he did not travel. If, on a Monday, he had to communicate with someone, he would jot down a few words on a piece of paper. Speaking less, he found he had more time for thought.

After a year of silence, Gandhi, now re-energized, found new ways to use satyagraha to achieve his goals. Women were encouraged to take part in civil disobedience. Gandhi gave them instructions for picketing liquor and foreign cloth shops. Volunteers were told to wear uniforms and carry banners "bearing warnings in bold letters." They should not use vulgarity or make threats: "The appeal must always be to the head and the heart, never to fear of force."

After the British decreed a large tax increase on the peasants in Bardoli, a town in Gujarat, he encouraged Sardar Vallabhbai Patel, a lawyer who had been the mayor of Ahmedabad, to lead a nonviolent protest. Patel asked the peasants to refuse to pay their taxes. The British government responded by confiscating their land and taking away their animals. Patel reminded the people they were fighting for a principle. The peasants refused to surrender and the government eventually conceded—returning the land and abolishing the tax increase. Gandhi called on all of India to mark the occasion and celebrate the success of satyagraha with a one-day hartal.

Demand for independence continued to mount, reaching fever pitch by the end of 1929. Jawaharlal Nehru was a barrister and a fervent admirer of Gandhi's—he now served as president of the Indian National Congress. He had studied at a boys' school outside London before attending Trinity College at Cambridge. Under Nehru's leadership, Congress passed a resolution in favor of complete independence from India—to be achieved by satyagraha. Civil disobedience would include nonpayment of taxes.

Gandhi was chosen to lead the satyagraha movement. Not sure what course to take, he waited for "an inner voice" to guide him. In February 1930 the revelation came to him—he would mount a large campaign against the salt tax and he would do all that he could to make the British aware of this unjust practice. The British had placed a high tax on salt and made it illegal to use salt not sold by the British government. Since all Indians used salt daily they were all were adversely affected by this tax.

On March 2, 1930, Gandhi sent a letter to the viceroy, Lord Irwin, stating that he found British rule to be "a curse." He believed that "progressive exploitation" and a "ruinous expensive military and civil administration" had reduced his people to serfdom. He pointed out that Lord Irwin's salary was 5,000 times India's average income. The British system was designed "to crush the very life out" of the poor person—one example being the salt on which all people depended. If Lord Irwin did not deal with the evils, he would disregard the provisions of the Salt Laws. Gandhi would risk arrest knowing there were "tens of thousands ready, in a disciplined manner, to take up the work after me." A British Quaker and sympathizer to the cause agreed to deliver Gandhi's letter. Lord Irwin sent no reply.

Ten days later, Gandhi and seventy-eight followers—men and women from the ashram—left Sabamarti and headed by foot to Dandi, a seacoast town 229 miles to the south. The march took twenty-four days. Each day, Gandhi walked between nine and ten miles, he spent an hour on the spinning wheel, and he wrote in his diary. In every village where Gandhi and his followers stopped crowds of people came out to greet them. Gandhi told them, "We are marching in the name of God." Many of those who gathered in the villages joined in and proceeded to the next village. By the time Gandhi arrived in Dandi the Salt March procession numbered several thousand.

On April 5, 1930, the day they reached their destination, Gandhi walked into the sea, put his hand in the water, and picked up some salt deposited by the waves. Gandhi was breaking the law—he touched salt which he had not purchased and on which he had not paid tax. His act was a dramatic and powerful protest that would resonate throughout the country.

Villagers along the coast followed Gandhi's example. They too waded into the ocean to collect salt—and as many as 60,000 were arrested,

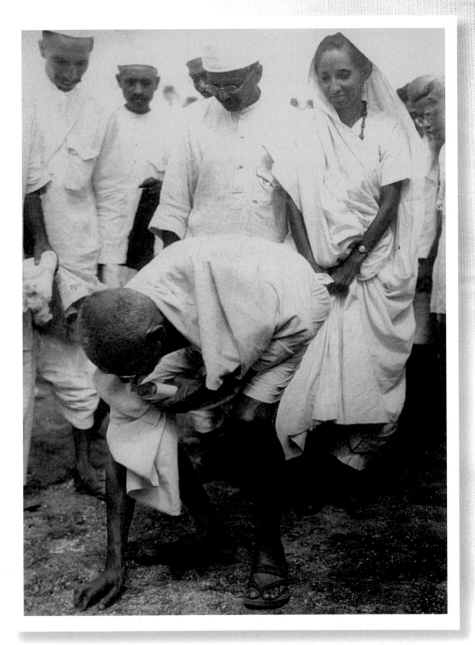

A photograph taken on April 5, 1930, of Gandhi breaking the salt
law by picking up a lump of natural salt in the village of Dandi in
Gujarat, India, at the end of the Salt March

including Gandhi's sons Ramdas and Devadas, as well as his assistant Mahadev Desai. Throughout India people continued to demonstrate. They made their own salt and refused to pay taxes. Gandhi expected he too would be arrested. It was a matter of time. The British stalled, not knowing whether Gandhi's arrest would put an end to the protest or lead to bloodshed. The British decided to risk arrest.

After midnight, on May 5, 1930, thirty Indian policemen arrived at Gandhi's camp outside Dandi. They entered his shed and found him sleeping. The men shone a flashlight in his face, awoke him, and announced that he was under arrest.

Gandhi was not sorry to go to jail—mass civil disobedience was working. Indians were becoming more self-sufficient. Britain was losing its hold. And the world was listening. People of all nations saw the injustice in the way Britain treated India. On May 17, 1930, Rabindrath Tagore wrote in the *Manchester Guardian* that England "is no longer regarded as the champion throughout the world of fair dealing, and the exponent of high principle, but as the upholder of Western race supremacy and the exploiter of those outside her own borders."

Indians, old and young, looked to Gandhi for guidance. Gandhi's Salt March had made history, and even in jail Gandhi could continue to inspire his country. "Little birds, ordinary birds cannot fly without wings," he wrote to the children in the ashram at Sabamarti. "With wings, of course, all can fly. But if you, without wings, will learn how to fly, then all your troubles will indeed be at an end. And I will teach you. See, I have no wings, yet I come flying to you every day in thought." He signed it, "Bapu's blessings."

Gandhi remained in jail until January 26, 1931—the day Congress issued a Declaration of Independence. India was not free, but she had shown that she could be. Lord Irwin announced that he would release Gandhi on the same day—Gandhi was determined to bring about a reconciliation and arranged to meet with the Viceroy at the new palace in Delhi.

During the next several weeks, Gandhi and Lord Irwin conferred many times, sometimes late into the night. On one occasion Lord

Irwin offered Gandhi tea. He accepted, pulled out a paper bag of salt, and said that he would add salt to his tea to remind them of the Boston Tea Party.

On March 5, after breakfast, the two leaders signed the Irwin-Gandhi Pact. Civil disobedience would stop. Although independence was not granted, Indian prisoners were freed, the British relinquished their control of salt manufacturing, and Congress would be allowed to attend the next Round Table Conference in London to discuss constitutional reforms. The prize was in sight.

When Gandhi arrived for the conference in London on September 12, 1931, he chose to stay in a settlement house in East London. He preferred to live among poor people where he would be accepted as a member of the family. In a radio address to the United States, he asked that people "give their hearty cooperation to India in her mighty struggle" and he hastened to add that the struggle would be nonviolent. "The world is sick unto death of blood-spilling." Gandhi added that India had other problems that needed to be addressed—the Hindu-Muslim conflict and the treatment of untouchables caused him "deep humiliation." He would not hide his country's flaws even while pleading for help.

Visitors from all over the world came to London to meet Gandhi. Vera Brittain, a pacifist and writer, who met Gandhi at a luncheon, recalled that "in deference to Gandhi's vegetarian principles, only fruit was served." Gandhi wore a loincloth and a khaddar cloak and spoke in a "thin, high voice." "With his small stature, toothless mouth, and spectacled eyes, he owed nothing to physical attraction; but no one ever needed it less." Gandhi's message was powerful and his warmth palatable.

Gandhi wore the same clothes (and sported a pocket watch) when he met with King George V and Queen Mary. Asked if he had enough on, he answered, "The King had enough on for both of us." Gandhi also met the actor Charlie Chaplin, the playwright George Bernard Shaw, and Dr. Maria Montessori, the physician who founded the Montessori method of education.

Gandhi on his way to meet Charlie Chaplin in London in September 1931

Winston Churchill, however, refused to see Gandhi. The British politician not only vehemently opposed Indian independence; he also disdained Gandhi and defamed his character. When Gandhi had met with Lord Irwin in Delhi, Churchill had described "the nauseating and humiliating spectacle" of a "lawyer now seditious fakir, striding half-naked up the steps of the Viceroy's palace, there to negotiate and to parley of equal terms with the representative of the King-Emperor." (A fakir is an Indian ascetic; the term can be used derogatorily to refer to a beggar.)

The Round Table Conference failed. Gandhi did not succeed in gaining greater constitutional reforms. Britain kept control of India's international relations and defense, as well as minority issues. The British favored the creation of a separate electorate (a body of qualified voters) for each of the different groups throughout India. (A Hindu electorate would vote for a Hindu representative, a Muslim electorate for a Muslim, a Sikh electorate for a Sikh. . . .) Gandhi, however, saw this as divisive and wanted no part of it. Discouraged and apprehensive about the future, he left London in December 1931.

On his way home Gandhi stopped in Switzerland to meet with the French author Romain Rolland, who had written a biographical sketch of Gandhi in 1924. In his book he had noted Gandhi's "infinite patience and infinite love," his "childlike simplicity," and his sincerity, comparing him to St. Francis of Assisi. Gandhi and Rolland spent a week together discussing politics, religion, art, music, their work and childhoods, nonviolence and the meaning of truth. Although they were meeting for the first time they were in many respects like brothers. But they had different views of God—Gandhi often said "Truth is God." Rolland, however, felt that Gandhi's God lacked "one important attribute"—joy. Rolland would not recognize a God without joy.

The sojourn in Switzerland was a pleasant interlude. But when Gandhi reached Bombay the atmosphere throughout the country was tense. Buildings had been seized, court trials and the writ of habeas corpus were suspended, and property was confiscated. Jawaharlal Nehru had been arrested. Gandhi protested Nehru's arrest—within days he too was arrested and put in the Yeravda central prison in Poona. (He was not alone. In January 1932, 14,800 persons were imprisoned.) The guards wanted to give Gandhi special treatment, but Gandhi refused their offers. He preferred to be treated like everyone else—he spent time at his spinning wheel, and tutored a prison official in Gujarati.

While in prison, Gandhi read in the newspapers that the proposal to create separate electorates for different groups had now become part of the British constitution for India. Gandhi argued that a separate electorate for the untouchables would only isolate them further from the rest of society. Such a plan was segregationist and discriminatory. Divisions between groups would deepen; far better to have one electorate for all Indians.

Gandhi started not by demanding a new constitution, but by building awareness of the status of the untouchables. He referred to them as "Harijans" meaning "children of God." On September 13, 1932, he announced that in an effort to fight prejudice and change attitudes towards the Harijans he would start a fast on Tuesday, September 20. Gandhi wrote the poet Tagore, "If your heart approves of the action I want your blessing." Tagore responded in a telegram, "It is worth sacrificing precious life for the sake of India's unity and her social integrity." Gandhi began his fast on September 20—newspapers gave the story extensive coverage.

Hindus opened twelve of their temples to the untouchables—thinking this might sway Gandhi from fasting. Jawaharlal Nehru's mother and thousands of Hindu women accepted food from untouchables. Hindus shared their water wells with untouchables; they sat together with untouchables. Resolutions to stop discrimination were passed.

Gandhi remained determined as he became weaker. His fasting was "a spiritual act" and "an intense prayer." His body pained him and he became nauseous. The story of Gandhi's fast traveled quickly—all across the country people shared in Gandhi's suffering. Kasturbai, who was being held prisoner in Sabarmati, was transferred to Yeravda and allowed to massage her husband's legs. By the fourth day, Gandhi's blood pressure had risen so high that the doctors believed he was close to death.

Hindus and Harijans tried to negotiate a settlement that would satisfy both parties—as well as Gandhi. The Harijans wanted separate primaries for Hindus and Harijans to be abolished after ten years— Gandhi suggested five years. The political leaders concluded that the date would be determined in later discussion—Gandhi was willing to accept the compromise. The British government announced that they too would agree to what became known as the Yeravda Pact.

On Monday, September 26, at 5:15 pm, Kasturbai gave Gandhi a sip of orange juice. The fast had made possible changes in the legislative procedure, and it accomplished far more than this: it altered forever the way in which untouchability was perceived. The difference in attitude was brought about not by the British government, nor the Indian Congress, but by the people throughout India whose hearts were moved by Gandhi's fast—and his willingness to risk his life.

CHAPTER EIGHT

The Soul
of a Nation

Gandhi remained in prison until May 8, 1933. After his release he continued to publish the *Harijan*, the weekly newspaper he had founded in prison. Gandhi wrote about exploitation and the need to become self-reliant. He described the gulf between the rich who lived in palaces and the poor who made homes of hovels. He offered practical advice on health and nutrition and used the paper to mount a campaign for every village to have a school, a theater, a public hall, clean wells, and electricity.

Ghanshyam Das Birla, a wealthy textile manufacturer, supported the newspaper and Gandhi's many other projects. He provided assistance for villages and the maintenance of the ashram. He also welcomed Gandhi into his home in Delhi—Gandhi often stayed for extended visits. Birla was devoted to Gandhi and wanted to help him in any way he could.

When Gandhi was asked "How is your family?" he answered, "All of India is my family." He had made friends with persons from all walks of life, rich and poor, educated and uneducated. He felt a natural affinity towards the Harijans, and he always had a special place in his heart for children. But he had never bonded with his sons, especially the two older boys. Their relationship had been fraught with tension. "I did not prove an ideal father," Gandhi wrote.

Gandhi was careful not to show any favoritism towards his own children—in fact he often over-compensated. He paid more attention to his cousins Maganlal and Chhaganlal—sending them to England to study although he had refused to send his own sons. Maganlal embraced Gandhi's principles, including brahmacharya. Working at the Phoenix settlement in South Africa and managing the ashram in Sabamarti, Maganlal had formed a deep attachment to the cousin who had become his spiritual adviser.

Gandhi's relationship with Maganlal underscored the neglect he showed his own sons. His son Manilal, at the age of twenty-four, had wanted to help his brother Harlilal set up a business in Calcutta. Manilal sent him money belonging to the ashram. When Gandhi discovered this, he immediately sent him away from the ashram. Manilal worked as an apprentice to a hand-spinner. After nine months his father still refused to welcome him back to the ashram and sent him to South Africa. Manilal found work as an editor of the *Indian Opinion*, the newspaper his father had founded. For many years Gandhi did not give his son permission to marry. Kasturbai finally persuaded him to relent but not until Manilal had reached the age of thirty-five.

Harilal, on the other hand, married when he was eighteen without his father's permission. Gandhi refused to support him and showed no respect for the path Harilal chose: "He wants to become rich, and that too easily. Possibly he has a grievance against me that when it was open to me to do so, I did not equip him and my other children for careers that lead to wealth and fame that wealth brings. . . . There is much in Harilal's life that I dislike. He knows that. But I love him in spite of his faults."

Kasturbai with her sons Devdas (top), Ramdas (left),
Manilal (right), and an unidentified woman and child

At the age of thirty, Harilal's wife died. He then started a commer-
cial business called All-India Stores, but he became an alcoholic and
was not a success. Kasturbai took in his four children and provided for
them. She rarely heard from her son. When she did the reports were
always disturbing. Harilal grew increasingly alienated from his father.
He converted to Islam and denounced his father in published letters
which he signed "Abdulla." Reconciliation did not seem possible.

Gandhi did not allow himself to show emotion. "It is not that I am incapable of anger, for instance," he wrote, "but I succeed on almost all occasions to keep my feelings under control. . . such a struggle leaves one stronger. . . . The more I work at this law the more I feel the delight in my life, the delight in the scheme of the universe." He believed there was "nothing that wastes the body like worry."

Gandhi also said he knew no hatred. "It is not non-violence if we love merely those that love us. It is non-violence only when we love those that hate us." Gandhi's views on nonviolence had become more deep-rooted.

As the 1930s wore on European dictators rose to power. Under Adolf Hitler, discrimination against Jews in Germany intensified—schools were segregated, books burned, shops shuttered, property confiscated, and synagogues destroyed. Benito Mussolini, the Fascist leader of Italy, who wanted his country to take over the world, invaded Ethiopia in 1936. In the Great Purge (1936-1938), Joseph Stalin, the Communist leader of the Soviet Union, accused party members and peasants of crimes—leading to their persecution, deportment, imprisonment, and execution.

Gandhi thought that Hitler, Mussolini, and Stalin could only be defeated by nonviolence. They had shown "the immediate effectiveness of violence"—it would take a miracle to right the situation. "All miracles are due to the silent and effective working of invisible force," he said. "Non-violence is the most invisible and the most effective."

In 1938, Nazi Germany annexed Austria and Czechoslovakia and, on September 1, 1939, Hitler invaded Poland. Two days later Britain declared war on Germany. Gandhi's sympathies lay with the Jews and the Allies and yet he could not condone the use of violence. "The tyrants of old never went so mad as Hitler seems to have done. If there ever could be a justifiable war in the name of and for humanity, war against Germany to prevent the wanton persecution of a whole race would be completely justified. But I do not believe in war," Gandhi wrote in the *Harijan* on November 11, 1938.

When Britain entered the war India too was pulled in—initially supplying 205,000 troops. Gandhi met with the viceroy and agreed not to undermine the Allied cause. However he would not support the use of violence. Members of the Indian Congress did not adopt Gandhi's pacifist stance and issued a statement that they would support the Allies only if and when India received her independence. But the position of Congress would not stop the growing number of army volunteers—by the end of the war they numbered 2.5 million. Indian forces fought in Southeast Asia, the Middle East, Africa, and Italy.

From September 7, 1940, to May 10, 1941, night after night, the Luftwaffe—the German air force—bombed London and other British cities. In what became known as the Blitz, 43,000 civilians were killed. Homes and landmarks, industrial targets and government offices were destroyed. Gandhi wrote to his disciple Madeleine Slade, now called Mirabchn: "The news about the destruction in England is heart-rending. The Houses of Parliament, the Abbey, the Cathedral seemed to be immortal."

On December 7, 1941, Japan bombed Pearl Harbor bringing the United States into the war. The next day the Japanese army invaded British Malaya (now Malaysia) and their navy attacked Singapore. Indian forces were defeated, British ships were sunk, and Allied aircraft destroyed.

Gandhi was convinced that Britain could not win the war unless India became free. "Britain is weaker and Britain is morally indefensible while she rules India," he said. On the one hand he advocated nonviolence, yet he also said that India could be used as a military base for the Allies, but only if she were to become free. He set in motion a "Quit India" campaign that would use nonviolent resistance. "The freedom of India means everything for us, but it means also much for the world. For freedom won through non-violence will mean the inauguration of a new order in the world."

Subhas Chandra Bose

Within the Indian National Congress, there were those who believed as Gandhi did, that British rule could be broken by peaceful means. But there were also young revolutionaries like Subhas Chandra Bose, who sought to break Great Britain's hold on India by violent means and with the help of foreign powers.

The son of a prominent and wealthy Bengali lawyer, Bose studied and passed the Indian Civil Service Examination at England's Cambridge University in 1919. But he didn't stay in the civil service long. He returned home to India in 1921, and joined Gandhi's movement, at the age of twenty-four.

He quickly rose in the ranks of the nationalist movement, and spent more than twenty years in the Indian National Congress. Twice he was elected and served as president (in 1938 and 1939), and in Indian politics his influence was exceeded only by Gandhi's and Nehru's. Between 1920 and 1941, Bose was jailed eleven times, for periods varying between six months and three years.

Eventually, however, Bose lost faith in Gandhi's strategies and began to advocate armed resistance against British authorities. Moreover, during World War II he formed the Indian National Army (also called the Azad Hind Fauj) and sought help from Nazi Germany and Japan in liberating India. In a May 1945 speech in Bangkok, he declared "Britain's enemy is India's friend." During the final two years of WWII—with considerable Japanese backing—he led forces of the Indian National Army into battle against the British.

Bose died under suspicious circumstances in 1945. Reportedly, he died of severe burns suffered in a plane crash in Taipei, Taiwan, on August 18. (A few days after Japan's announced surrender in August 1945, he was said to have fled Southeast Asia.) However, Bose's body was never recovered, and millions of Indians believed that he lived well into the 1970s. Three separate commissions have studied what happened to Bose, yet the debate about his mysterious death continues. Taiwanese authorities have said there was no such crash in Taipei in August 1945.

Throughout his political career, Bose advocated for complete independence from Great Britain, and he believed that there could be no compromise. Also, he absolutely rejected the idea that India should be partitioned. A few days after his death, Jawaharlal Nehru said:

> In the struggle for the cause of India's independence he has given his life and has escaped all those troubles which brave soldiers like him have to face in the end. He was not only brave but had deep love for freedom. He believed, rightly or wrongly, that whatever he did was for the independence of India . . . Although I personally did not agree with him in many respects, and he left us and formed the Forward Bloc, nobody can doubt his sincerity. He struggled throughout his life for the independence of India, in his own way.

Though Western historians routinely describe Bose as a traitor and fascist collaborator for seeking aid from the Axis powers, Bose is popularly known as Netaji, or "revered leader" in India. He has been immortalized in film, with the 2005 movie *Netaji Subhas Chandra Bose: The Forgotten Hero.* And, according to one of his many biographers, Mihir Bose (no relation), Bose's name "is given [in India] to parks, roads, buildings, sports stadiums, artificial lakes; his statues stand in place of those of discarded British heroes and his photograph adorns thousands of calendars and millions of pan (betel-nut) shops."

Gandhi with Congress president Subhas Chandra Bose at the 1938 Indian National Congress annual meeting

Prime Minister Winston Churchill opposed freeing India and wanted to win the war without granting her independence. President Franklin Roosevelt tried to dissuade him—and failed. Churchill boldly proclaimed, "I have not become the King's First Minister in order to preside at the liquidation of the British Empire." Gandhi could not resist a touch of humor; in a letter to Churchill he referred to the name-calling from his previous visit to London, "You are reported to have the desire to crush the 'naked fakir'. . . I have been long trying to be a fakir and that, naked—a more difficult task. I therefore regard the expression as a compliment, though unintended. . . . [I] ask you to trust and use me for the sake of your people and mine and through them those of the world."

Churchill sent Sir Stafford Cripps, a member of his War Cabinet who had served as British ambassador to Russia, to New Delhi to negotiate with Indian leaders. Cripps arrived on March 22, 1942, and met with Gandhi to present his proposal. Although the British plan allowed for the creation of an Indian "Dominion," a self-governing state that

Gandhi standing with British parliamentarian
Sir Stafford Cripps in Delhi, India, in March 1942

could vote itself out of the British Commonwealth, it also gave autonomy to Indian princes in provinces that were heavily influenced by the British. Both Gandhi and Congress refused Cripps's offer—believing it would leave India divided.

In August 1942, members of Congress again convened to discuss India's freedom. This time they called for the end of British rule and said that if freedom were granted they would agree to the stationing of the Allied Armed Forces in India. However, if the resolution was not accepted they would plan a civil disobedience campaign under Gandhi's leadership. Gandhi asked the delegates to wait for the viceroy's response, and he urged the viceroy to accept the resolution.

But there was no time to persuade the viceroy. Before dawn on August 8, 1942, Gandhi, his good friend and assistant Mahadev Desai, Nehru, and others were arrested and imprisoned. Kasturbai, now seventy-four, volunteered to speak at the meeting in Bombay where her husband had planned to speak. She too was arrested and joined Gandhi in the prison at Yeravda. Gandhi had never succeeded in teaching his wife to read and write; he renewed his efforts while they were in prison, and also included lessons in geography.

Outside the prison violence erupted. Buildings were set on fire and property was destroyed and government workers were attacked. Gandhi and the viceroy exchanged long letters. The viceroy blamed Gandhi for the violence—Gandhi blamed the British government. He announced that he would fast for twenty-one days to try to persuade the British to relinquish their power.

People from across the country demanded the government free Gandhi. The British did not want to be held responsible if he were to die in prison, and they offered to release him for the duration of the fast. Gandhi insisted he remain in prison, and he began his fast on February 10, 1943. He took water but without salt or fruit juice; every day he grew weaker and suffered from nausea. His kidneys began to fail. The doctors insisted that intravenous feeding was needed to save his life, but Gandhi refused.

Gandhi received numerous visitors, including his two younger sons Devadas and Ramdas. Kasturbai prayed for her husband—and on March 2 he ended his fast. Kasturbai gave him his first sips of orange juice. The government continued to blame Gandhi for the outbreak of violence.

Slowly Gandhi recovered. Mahadev Desai had died in prison of a heart attack, and Gandhi and Kasturbai had mourned his loss. Now Kasturbai's health was failing. In December 1943, her bronchitis worsened and she grew critically ill. She was allowed to receive visits from her sons and grandsons. She asked for Harilal. Her head was resting on Gandhi's lap when she died.

Gandhi and Kasturbai had spent sixty-two years together. "I cannot imagine life without her," he said. Their relationship, once contentious, had changed over time. His bond and his loyalty had deepened. "Her determined resistance to my will on the one hand, and her quiet submission to the suffering my stupidity involved on the other, ultimately made me ashamed of myself and cured me of my stupidity in thinking that I was born to rule over her, and in the end she became my teacher in non-violence."

Gandhi paid tribute to the role Kasturbai played in sharing his life's work. "Whatever place our women have achieved today is due to Kasturbai's courage, purity and steadfast faith. She might have been a totally uneducated woman, but she possessed all the virtues which a woman should have. On the strength of these virtues, India and I have risen high. I do not hesitate to say the country or any of her citizens can hardly repay the debt."

Shortly after Kasturbai's death, an attack of malaria caused Gandhi to become delirious, yet at first he resisted taking medicine. His fruit-juice diet failed—he agreed to take quinine and recovered. His doctors reported severe anemia and low blood pressure. The people of India called for his release, and on May 6, 1944 he was freed.

Kasturbai Gandhi died on February 22, 1944

Gandhi renewed his efforts to create a unified India. He reached out to Mohammad Ali Jinnah, head of the Muslim League, in an effort to persuade him that the states and provinces where Muslims constituted a majority should not secede from the Indian Union. Jinnah, however, favored secession and wanted to form a new country in the region that is now Pakistan.

On August 14, 1945, Japan surrendered to the Allied Powers after two atomic bombs were dropped on the country. Germany had already surrendered. There was much rebuilding to be done. Great Britain had

The Japanese surrendered after atomic bombs were dropped on two of its cities. Nagasaki was reported to be "like a graveyard with not a tombstone standing." In response to the attack and the merciless destruction Gandhi said, "Mankind has to get out of violence only through non-violence. Hatred can be overcome only by love."

won the war but she could not provide the resources to keep India in check. Independence was no longer in question, but the subject of unity was unresolved. The British Labor Party, now in power, prepared to recognize self-government in India and sent a Cabinet mission to Delhi to negotiate the terms.

To Gandhi the idea of partition of Muslims and Hindus was blasphemous. They both shared a common heritage and culture and were mutually dependent on each other. Their transportation and communication systems as well as their daily lives were inextricably linked. All his life he had worked for the "oneness of the human family. Therefore, those who want to divide India into possibly warring groups are enemies alike of India and Islam," he wrote in the *Harijan*.

In August 1946 the British viceroy called on Jawaharlal Nehru and members of the Congress to form a new government. Nehru asked Jinnah, head of the Muslim League, to participate, but the Muslim leader refused. On September 2, 1946, Nehru was named prime minister of India. Jinnah wanted no part of the new government and proclaimed a day of mourning. Fighting broke out in Bombay and in the Punjab. Gandhi called on both groups, Hindu and Muslim, to stop the violence and he pleaded with them to strive for peace and a sense of security without relying on the British for protection.

But the attacks continued. Gandhi was asked if he still favored nonviolence. "The failure of my technique of non-violence causes no loss of faith in non-violence itself," he wrote in the *Harijan*. Muslims attacked Hindus in Noakhali, a district in Bengal. In the Bihar, one of the eastern states where the Hindus outnumbered the Muslims six to one, the people called for revenge and a "Noakhali Day" was declared. A riot ensued with Hindus shouting "Blood for blood." Gandhi estimated that more than 10,000 died.

Between November 7, 1946, and March 2, 1947, Gandhi walked barefoot from village to village in the predominantly Muslim Noakhali region. He stopped in forty-nine villages to talk and pray with the people—trying to bring peace and make it possible for the Hindus to return to the homes they had abandoned.

Jawaharlal Nehru with Gandhi

Millions of Hindus and Sikhs left the Punjab region, which would become an area that is still contested between India and Pakistan, and crossed into the Indian Union. At the same time millions of Muslims fled the Indian Union for Pakistan. Nehru's government set up camps for both groups outside New Delhi. Gandhi visited both Hindu and Muslim camps. All that he saw—people who had fled from their homes, those who were sick and had no food, the ones who were dying—weighed on him.

In November 1946, British prime minister Clement Atlee summoned Nehru and Jinnah to London. He wanted Jinnah to renounce partition, but the mission failed. Nehru and the Indian National Congress voted to allow parts of India to accept the newly proposed constitution—thus facilitating the division of the country. Gandhi did not favor this decision. Although Nehru looked up to Gandhi as a father he was not afraid to speak his own mind.

On February 20, 1947, Prime Minister Atlee announced that England would leave India no later than June 1948. Lord Louis Mountbatten, a British admiral and a great grandson of Queen Victoria, would replace Archibald Wavell as viceroy—Mountbatten would become the last in a line of British rulers stretching back almost a century. Lord Mountbatten and his wife, Lady Edwina, arrived in New Delhi on March 22, 1947. Edwina Mountbatten, a wealthy heiress, had led a glamorous and often frivolous life before the war. Once in India, she entertained regally, befriended the leaders of the Indian independence movement, and devoted herself to relief work.

While Lady Edwina tended to orphan children and those who were sick in refugee camps, her husband held long meetings with both Gandhi and Jinnah. Mountbatten thought it best to speed up the timetable for independence so that the fighting and rioting would stop. He favored a united India, but was convinced that Jinnah would never accept this and partition was necessary to avoid civil war. It was a view Gandhi did not share, but one Mountbatten came to after thoughtful deliberation. If partition were to occur the Punjab and Bengal areas would need to be divided so that parts that were predominantly Hindu could remain with the Indian Union. Jinnah preferred to keep the provinces intact, but Mountbatten saw no other way to end the conflict.

Riots continued to pit Hindus against Muslims. Houses were burned—temples and mosques were destroyed. Killings increased. Mountbatten flew to London to discuss India's future. His plan was not perfect but he considered it better than the alternatives. Prime Minister Atlee accepted the Mountbatten plan, provided the Congress agree to it.

Sardar Vallabhbhai Patel, a leader in the Congress, favored Mountbatten's plan and urged Nehru and the Congress to accept it. He also encouraged the representatives of the country's princely kingdoms to join the Indian Union. Pressure mounted as the violence grew more rampant. On June 15, 1947, the Congress voted for the plan—despite Gandhi's wishes. Mountbatten saw no reason to delay India's independence and arranged for the transition to take place sooner than originally planned. He hoped the change in date would assure a peaceful resolution.

At midnight on August 14, 1947, ten months ahead of schedule, India achieved her independence. The delegates in the Constituent Assembly Hall in New Delhi came from many races and cultures, and religions. They wore khaddars, saris, and princely robes. Prime Minister Nehru addressed them all:

> A moment comes, which comes but rarely in history, when we step out from the old to the new, when an age ends, and when the soul of a nation, long suppressed, finds utterance. . . . We end today a period of ill fortune and India discovers herself again. . . . Freedom and power bring responsibility. The responsibility rests upon this Assembly, a sovereign body representing the sovereign people of India.

From the gallery overlooking the hall a man blew from a conch shell, a long plaintive sound full of promise, an ancient ritual that signaled a new age. Outside a clap of thunder was heard—and the rain poured down.

CHAPTER NINE

"No Ordinary Light"

The India that had been controlled by the British Raj was now divided into two countries: Pakistan and the Indian Union. Pakistan included the Punjab, Sind, the Northwest Frontier, and Baluchistan, all to the northwest, and on the other side of India, East Bengal. The other former states and provinces, the former princely states, made up the Indian Union. But the partition failed to provide peace or stability. Fear and uncertainty over the future led to increased fighting and destruction.

Jinnah, the longtime advocate of Indian Muslim rights who had served as leader of the Muslim League, was named governor-general of Pakistan. He could not stop the thousands of Hindus from fleeing Pakistan. Meanwhile, Delhi was overcome by violence. Prime Minister Nehru and Deputy Prime Minister Patel were stymied—they could neither control the violence nor plan for feeding and sheltering of the refugees. Nehru and Patel greatly admired Lord Mountbatten—they had tremendous respect for his leadership and judgment. In a secret meeting they asked Mountbatten not only to advise them, but to

Governor-general Lord Mountbatten and Lady Mountbatten
with Nehru (middle right) in New Delhi, India, on June 19, 1948

also become governor-general of the Indian Union. Mountbatten was
stunned. He had never expected to be asked to stay in India. He hesi-
tated—briefly—and then agreed. Nehru and Patel formed an Emer-
gency Committee and expressed great relief when Mountbatten took
the helm.

Gandhi remained in Calcutta during the celebration of independence. He was in no mood to celebrate. The violence that had erupted
throughout the country distressed him. He didn't think the partition
would stop the conflict. The new leaders of the two countries, Nehru,
Patel, and Jinnah, were his close friends, yet he had been unable to
persuade them to avoid partition.

His stance against partition was controversial. On August 31, 1947,
two weeks after independence, rioters broke into the house where he
was staying. One of them threw a brick and another swung a stick at
him. Gandhi, unharmed, knew he must summon all his strength to

bring peace to the city. He vowed to fast until the people of Calcutta pledged to stop the fighting. He hoped his fast would touch their hearts and give them the courage to refrain from violence. Hindu, Muslim, and Christian representatives from all walks of life visited Gandhi to assure him that their city would remain peaceful. Gandhi insisted on a written promise. On September 4, the delegates presented him with their pledge. At 9:15 pm he took a sip of lime juice.

Gandhi moved on to Delhi thinking his presence there might help. He met with leaders from different factions and aided and comforted the refugees who had settled in camps in and around the city. After partition, 15 million men, women, and children would seek new homes; Hindus and Sikhs left Pakistan to come to the Indian Union; Muslims left the Indian Union for Pakistan. All feared for their lives as they made their escape. Outside Delhi the refugees walked in a line fifty-seven miles long. Babies and toddlers had to be carried. Those who were too weak to walk, the aged and the sick, were often abandoned by the side of the road. In the camps, food was scarce and disease was widespread.

"Where do congratulations come in? Would it not be more appropriate to send condolences?" Gandhi asked on October 2, 1947, as he opened hundreds of telegrams from around the world. It was his seventy-eighth birthday. "There is nothing but anguish in my heart." Gandhi's people loved him, yet his wisdom eluded them.

Skirmishes erupted in Kashmir, the region to the north of India bordering Pakistan and Tibet. Both Indian and Pakistani troops battled over the annexation of Kashmir. Gandhi recommended mediation or a referendum, but the fighting continued. In October 1947, the maharajah of Kashmir, Hari Singh, asked that his kingdom become part of the Indian Union.

Violence within the Indian Union subsided, yet the hostility between religious groups still remained high. On January 13, 1948, Gandhi, who had settled into G. D. Birla's home in New Delhi, started a fast to help heal the differences between Hindus and Muslims. His friends feared the fast would kill him, but his decision—a sudden one—made him happy. Various committees met to find creative ways to assure there would be peace.

Gandhi lost weight rapidly; on the third day he weighed only 107 pounds. Water made him nauseous. In the morning he lay in a stupor, but by 5 pm, he had become alert and wanted to pray. It was arranged that he would speak through a microphone and that his words would be broadcast. "Each of us should turn the searchlight inward and purify his or her heart as much as possible," he said, speaking to both Hindus and Muslims.

On the fourth day of the fast, he again broadcast his prayer. The next day Nehru came to see him. He thought Gandhi was dying and his eyes filled with tears. Telegrams arrived from leaders all across India. Meanwhile delegates from various organizations and refugee groups met with Dr. Rajendra Prasad, president of the Congress, to make pledges for peace with concrete plans for implementation.

On January 18, 1948, one hundred delegates came to the Birla house in New Delhi to present their pledge of peace. Gandhi was promised that Muslims would be welcome in Delhi, that they would be able to conduct business, and that their mosques would be returned to them. But Gandhi still was not satisfied—he wanted reconciliation not only in Delhi but throughout India.

Muslim scholars, the ambassador from Pakistan, and a Sikh representative came forward to assure him of their commitment to friendship between Hindus, Muslims, Sikhs, Christians, Parsis, and Jews. Gandhi sat quietly. After a long silence, he said he would break the fast.

Religious rioting in Pakistan and the Indian Union came to a halt. Gandhi was filled with hope that the promise of friendship between Hindus and Muslims boded well for the relationship between India and Pakistan. The two countries were inextricably bound the one to the other. "If there is darkness in the Union, it would be folly to expect light in Pakistan. But if the night in the Union is dispelled beyond the shadow of a doubt, it cannot be otherwise in Pakistan," he wrote to Mirabehn.

Gandhi was showing signs of age. He had become dependent on his two grand-nieces, Abha and Manu. Every evening they accompanied him to a prayer meeting, supporting him as he walked. During one meeting, a few days after the fast ended, a young man threw a grenade into the crowd. Gandhi, his life spared, showed no anger towards the youth—wishing only that he could help him mend his ways. Gandhi knew what he had just witnessed would not be the last attempt made on his life: "An assassin's bullet may put an end to my life. I would welcome it. But I would love, above all, to fade out doing my duty with my last breath."

On January 30, 1948, Gandhi was on his way to his usual prayer meeting. He had stopped to talk and was running late. Abha chided him, "Bapu, your watch must be feeling very neglected. You would not look at it." Gandhi answered, "Why should I, since you are my time-keepers?"

Nathuram Vinayak Godse, the Brahmin editor of a Hindu weekly newspaper, had come to the prayer meeting. He was angry that Gandhi had made concessions to the Muslims and that Muslims were allowed to participate in Hindu services. Manu noticed Godse pushing his way through the crowd. He bumped into her and made her drop the things she was carrying—a notebook, prayer beads, and Gandhi's spittoon. He bowed to Gandhi and Gandhi bowed in return.

Godse removed a pistol from his pocket and shot Gandhi three times. His white garments turned red with blood. The man of peace had been assassinated.

It fell to Prime Minister Nehru to address the nation by radio:

> Friends and comrades, the light has gone out of our lives
> and there is darkness everywhere. I do not know what
> to tell you and how to say it. Our beloved leader, Bapu
> as we called him, the father of the nation, is no more. . . .

Gandhi's second-youngest son, Ramdas,
lights his father's funeral pyre on January 31, 1948

The light has gone out, I said, and yet I was wrong. For the light that shone in this country was no ordinary light. The light that has illumined this country for these many years will illumine this country for many more years, and a thousand years later that light will still be seen in this country, and the world will see it and it will give solace to innumerable hearts.

More than 1.5 million people joined the funeral procession and walked together to the Jumna River. Rose petals were strewn along the path. Another million people, Indians of all religions, most dressed in white, waited at the river's edge. They watched as Gandhi's son Ramdas set fire to the funeral pyre where Gandhi's body, adorned with garlands of oleander and white jasmine, was placed. The body went up in flames and the logs from the pyre burned for fourteen hours. Later the ashes were divided into fifty portions and distributed to friends and family, many of them immersed into India's sacred rivers as was Hindu custom.

On January 30, 2010, six decades after Gandhi's assassination, his granddaughter, Ela Gandhi, scattered some of his ashes off the coast of South Africa. It was here in this country that her grandfather had confronted discrimination and developed some of his philosophies of peaceful resistance—here too that Nelson Mandela, the first black president of South Africa, had once remarked, "India gave us Barrister Gandhi and South Africa gave back Mahatma Gandhi the great soul."

TIMELINE

1869:   Born October 2 in Porbandar, a city on the western coast of India.

1883:   Marries Kasturbai Majanki.

1888:   Sets sail for England to become a barrister.

1893:   Arrives in Durban, South Africa, to practice law.

1894:   Organizes Natal Indian Congress.

1899:   Forms Indian Ambulance Corps during Second Boer War.

1903:   Publishes *Indian Opinion* and founds Phoenix settlement near Durban.

1906:   Starts satyagraha movement after passage of the Black Act.

1910:   Establishes communal living at Tolstoy Farm near Johannesburg.

1913:   Leads march from Newcastle mines in Natal to the Transvaal; arrested.

1914:   Sails to England after General Smuts concedes and passage of Indian Relief Act.

1915:   Establishes satyagraha ashram near Ahmedabad; becomes leader of Indian National Congress.

1917:   Starts Champaran campaign to protect indigo workers.

1919:   Organizes nationwide hartal; suspends satyagraha after Himalayan miscalculation; investigates Amritsar massacre.

1920:   Named president of All-India Home Rule League; campaigns for swaraj (self-governance).

1922:   Arrested and charged with sedition; sentenced to six years' imprisonment.

1924:   Starts twenty-one day fast to encourage Hindu-Muslim friendship.

1930:   Leads 229-mile Salt March to Dandi.

1931:   Signs Irwin-Gandhi Pact paving way towards independence.

1932:   Begins fast to draw attention to treatment of untouchables.

1933:   Founds weekly paper, the *Harijan*; raises status of the untouchables.

1942:   Organizes "Quit India" campaign.

1944:   Wife of sixty-two years, Kasturbai, dies in prison.

1947:   Opposes partition after India gains independence.

1948:   Begins last fast to foster peace between Hindus and Muslims.

1948:   Assassinated at evening prayer meeting.

SOURCES

CHAPTER ONE: Indian Roots

p. 9,   "we are a weak . . ." M. K. Gandhi, *An Autobiography or The Story of My Experiments with Truth*, trans. Mahadev Desai (Ahmedabad, India: Navajivan Publishing House, 1927), 20.

p. 9,   "Behold the mighty Englishman . . ." Ibid., 21.

p. 10,   "it would make me strong . . ." Ibid.

p. 15,   "bad company," Ibid., 19.

p. 15,   "I know he has the weakness . . ." Ibid.

p. 16,   "a tragedy," Ibid.

p. 16,   "dark days," Ibid., 25.

p. 19,   "the brightest jewel in the crown," "Imperialism to Postcolonialism-Perspectives on the British empire: Overview," http://www.wwnorton.com/college/english/nael/20century/topic_1/welcome.htm.

CHAPTER THREE: Setting the Stage

p. 32,   "The ordinary Coolie . . ." *Reader's Digest Illustrated History of South Africa. The Real Story*, 3rd ed. (Cape Town, South Africa: The Reader's Digest Association South Africa, 1994), 224.

p. 33,   "merchant menace," Ibid., 274.

p. 35,   "I refuse to get . . ." Mohandas K. Gandhi, *An Autobiography*, 111.

p. 35,   "The hardship to which . . ." Ibid., 112.

p. 35,   "I was ashamed . . ." Ibid., 99.

p. 37,   "love your enemies . . ." *New International Version Bible* (Luke 6:27).

p. 37,   "the infinite possibilities . . ." Gandhi, *An Autobiography*, 160.

p. 37,   "True non-resistance is the one . . ." Leo Tolstoy, *The Kingdom of God Is Within You*, trans. Leo Wiener (New York: Noonday Press, 1961), 19.

pp. 37-38,   "Slavery was contrary . . ." Ibid., 138-139.

p. 38,   "it has existed . . . away from it," Ibid., 198.

p. 39,   "but our innermost prayer. . . the same goal?" Mahatma Gandhi, *The Essential Gandhi: An Anthology of His Writings on His Life, Work, and Ideas*, ed. Louis Fischer (New York: Vintage Books, 2002), 184.

p. 40,   "The true function . . ." Gandhi, *An Autobiography*, 134.

p. 40,   "I wanted to reserve . . . beauty of compromise," Ibid., 147-148.

p. 41,   "Such service can . . ." Ibid., 175.

CHAPTER FOUR: Self-Reliance

p. 45,   "I do not at all like . . . " Gandhi, *An Autobiography*, 191.

p. 46,   "We'll hang old Gandhi . . ." Reader's Digest Illustrated History of South Africa, 274.

p. 47,   "the school of experience . . ." Ibid., 200.

p. 47,   "constant contact," Ibid.

p. 47,   "A child, before it . . ." M. K. Gandhi, *Non-Violent Resistance (Satyagraha)*, (Mineoloa, New York: Dover Publications, 2001), 36.

p. 48,   "Have you no sense . . ." Gandhi, *An Autobiography*, 277.

p. 49,   "The voice of the people . . ." Ibid., 219.

p. 49,   "service was its own . . ." Ibid., 220.

p. 49,   "costly ornaments . . ." Ibid.

p. 50,   "rest in peace . . ." Ibid., 240.

p. 50,   "hate the sin . . ." Ibid., 276.

p. 51,   "life worth living . . ." Ibid., 299.

p. 52,   "existed for the welfare . . ." Gandhi, *An Autobiography*, 313.

p. 53,   "My heart was with . . ." Ibid., 314.

p. 53,   "Kaffirs are as a rule . . ." David Arnold and Stuart H. Blackburn, eds., *Telling Lives in India: Biography, Autobiography and Life History* (Bloomington, IN: Indiana University Press, 2004), 34.

p. 53,   "Many of the native . . ." Rory Carroll, "Gandhi branded racist as Johannesburg honours freedom fighter," *Guardian* (UK), October 17, 2003.

p. 56,   "horrors of war . . ." Gandhi, *An Autobiography*, 315.

p. 56,   "with his whole soul . . ." Ibid., 316.

p. 56,   "a helpmate, a comrade . . ." Ibid., 278.

p. 56,   "a life of contentment . . ." Ibid., 279.

p. 57,   "lie by the side . . ." Avind Kala, "The Mahatma and his 'girls,'" *Free Press* (Mumbai, India) *Journal*, January 12, 1997.

CHAPTER FIVE: Satyagraha in South Africa

p. 59,   "saw nothing in it . . ." Mohandas K. Gandhi, *Satyagraha in South Africa*, trans. Valji Govindji Desai (Ahmedabad: Navajivan Publishing House, 1928), 92.

p. 60,   "so long as there is . . ." Ibid., 99.

p. 60,   "A satyagrahi. . ." Gandhi, *Non-Violent Resistance*, 77.

p. 61,   "Every Indian knows . . ." Ibid., 123.

p. 61,   "suffer peacefully . . ." Gandhi, *Satyagraha in South Africa*, 125.

p. 63,   "No cowardly fear . . ." Ibid., 156.

p. 63,   "By burning the certificates . . ." Ibid., 186.

p. 64,   "how deep [were] the ruts . . ." Henry David Thoreau, *Walden* (London: George Routledge & Sons, 1904), 249.

p. 64,   "Rather than love . . ." Ibid., 254.

pp. 64-65, "I have often felt . . . to do first," Louis Fischer, *The Life of Mahatma Gandhi*. (London: Harper Collins, 1950), 121.

p. 67,   "the growth of crime . . ." Leo Nikolayevich Tolstoy, *Correspondence of Tolstoy* (Sydney, Australia: Accessible Publishing Systems, ReadHowYouWant Classics Library, 2008), 94.

p. 69,   "I will not break . . ." Gandhi, *Satyagraha in South Africa*, 273.

pp. 69, 72, "General Smuts too saw . . ." Ibid., 291.

p. 72,   "A Satyagrahi fights . . ." Ibid., 298.

p. 73,   "Satyagraha is a priceless . . ." Ibid., 307.

CHAPTER SIX: Swaraj in India

p. 75,   "participation in war . . ." Gandhi, *An Autobiography*, 349.

p. 79,   "Justice demands . . ." Jabez T. Sunderland, "The New Nationalist Movement in India," *Atlantic*, October 1908, http://www.theatlantic.com/magazine/archive/1969/12/the-new-nationalist-movement-in-India/4893/

p. 79,   "Perhaps the greatest . . ." Ibid.

p. 82,   "As a law-abiding citizen . . . penalty of disobedience," Gandhi, *An Autobiography*, 413.

p. 82,   "irritate . . . gentleness," Ibid., 418.
p. 83,   "remain firm . . ." Ibid., 427.
p. 83,   "Unless the strikers . . ." Ibid., 431.
p. 83,   "thunderstruck . . ." Ibid.
p. 83,   "the outward gentleness . . ." Ibid., 437.
p. 83,   "an inborn gentleness . . ." Ibid.
p. 85,   "in that twilight condition . . . " Ibid., 459.
p. 85,   "perfect peace . . ." Gandhi, *An Autobiography*, 464.
p. 88,   "delirious with joy . . ." Ibid., 476.
p. 88,   "to what lengths . . ." Ibid., 477.
p. 89,   "true resistance . . . to withhold cooperation," Ibid., 482.
p. 89,   "intensely active . . . ill-will or hatred," Gandhi, *Non-Violent Resistance*, 162-163.
p. 90,   "curse of untouchability," Gandhi, *Autobiography*, 502.
p. 90,   "It is a sin . . ." Mahatma Gandhi, *The Essential Gandhi: An Anthology of His Writings on His Life, Work, and Ideas*, ed. Louis Fischer (New York: Vintage Books, 2002), 118-119.
p. 91,   "How can . . . cooperation with good," Gandhi, *The Essential Gandhi*, 256-259.

CHAPTER SEVEN: "Love Never Claims"
p. 94,   "Make our hearts . . . " Gandhi, *The Essential Gandhi*, 162-163.
p. 94,   "For me, the spinning . . . " Ibid., 195.
pp. 94-95, "I own no property . . ." Ibid., 268.
p. 96,   "You shall be . . ." Mirabehn (Madeleine Slade), *Gandhi's Letters to a Disciple* (New York: Harper & Brothers, 1950), 10.
p. 96,   "Bapu was full of love. . ." Ibid., 231.
p. 96,   "My attitude towards . . . themselves responsible," Gandhi, *The Essential Gandhi*, 167-168.
p. 96,   "It has often . . ." Ibid., 207.
p. 97,   "bearing warnings . . ." Gandhi, *Non-Violent Resistance*, 335.
p. 97,   "The appeal . . ." Ibid.
p. 98,   "a curse . . . work after me," Gandhi, *The Essential Gandhi*, 225-227.
p. 98,   "We are marching . . ." Ibid., 227.
p. 100,   "is no longer regarded…" Ibid., 229.
p. 100,   "Little birds . . . Bapu's blessings," Ibid., 228.
p. 101,   "give their hearty . . . deep humiliation," Ibid., 230.
p. 101,   "in deference to Gandhi's . . . needed it less," Vera Brittain, *Search After Sunrise* (London: Macmillan & Co., 1951), 22.
p. 101,   "The King had enough . . ." Gandhi, *The Essential Gandhi*, 233.
p. 102,   "the nauseating . . . the King-Emperor," Ibid., 229-230.
p. 103,   "infinite patience . . . childlike simplicity," Romain Rolland, *Mahatma Gandhi: The Man Who Became One with the Universal Being*, trans. Catherine D. Groth (New Delhi: Publications Division, 1924), 1.
p. 103,   "Truth is God . . . one important attribute," Fischer, *The Life of Mahatma Gandhi*, 368.
p. 104,   "If your heart . . . social integrity," Gandhi, *The Essential Gandhi*, 241.
p. 104,   "a spiritual act," Gandhi, *Non-Violent Resistance*, 315.
p. 104,   "an intense prayer," Ibid.

CHAPTER EIGHT: The Soul of a Nation

p. 108,   "How is your family . . ." Gandhi, *The Essential Gandhi*, 156.

p. 108,   "I did not prove an ideal father," M. K. Gandhi, *An Autobiography*, 311.

p. 108,   "He wants to become rich . . ." Gandhi, *The Essential Gandhi*, 157.

p. 110,   "It is not that . . . like worry," Ibid., 276-277.

p. 110,   "It is not non-violence . . ." Ibid., 289.

p. 110,   "the immediate effectiveness . . . the most effective," Ibid., 289.

pp. 110-111,   "The tyrants of old . . ." Fischer, *The Life of Mahatma Gandhi*, 433.

p. 111,   "The news about . . . " Gandhi, *The Essential Gandhi*, 300.

p. 111,   "Britain is weaker . . ." Fischer, *The Life of Mahatma Gandhi*, 469.

p. 111,   "The freedom of India . . ." Gandhi, *The Essential Gandhi*, 304.

p. 112,   "Britain's enemy is . . ." Ranjan Borra, "Subhas Chandra Bose, The Indian National Army, and the War of India's Liberation," *Journal of Historical Review* 3, no. 4 (Winter 1982): 407-439, www.ihr.org/jhr/v03/v03p407_Borra.html.

p. 113,   "In the struggle . . ." Ibid.

p. 113,   "is given [in India] . . ." Ibid.

p. 114,   "I have not become . . . those of the world," Gandhi, *The Essential Gandhi*, 301.

p. 116,   "I cannot imagine . . . teacher in non-violence," Ibid., 305.

p. 116,   "Whatever place . . . ." Mahatma Gandhi, *The Collected Works of Mahatma Gandhi*, vol. XC, November 11, 1947-January 30, 1948 (New Delhi: The Publications Division, 1958-1984), 121.

p. 119,   "like a graveyard . . ." Donald M. Goldstein, Katherine V. Dillon, and J. Michael Wenger, *Rain of Ruin: A Photographic History of Hiroshima and Nagasaki* (Washington: Brassey's, 1995), 94.

p. 119,   Mankind has to get out of violence . . ." Gandhi, *The Essential Gandhi*, 293-4.

p. 120,   "oneness of the human . . ." Ibid., 308.

p. 120,   "The failure of my technique . . ." Ibid., 311.

p. 123,   "A moment comes . . ." Jawaharlal Nehru, *Jawaharlal Nehru's Speeches*, Vol. 1. Sept 1946-May 1949 (New Delhi: Publications Division, 1949), 25.

CHAPTER NINE: "No Ordinary Light"

p. 127,   "Where do congratulations . . . in my heart." Gandhi, *The Essential Gandhi*, 317.

p. 128,   "Each of us should turn the searchlight . . ." Ibid., 318.

pp. 128-129,   "If there is darkness . . ." Ibid., 321.

p. 129,   "An assassin's bullet . . ." Ibid., 318.

p. 129,   "Bapu, your watch . . . you are my time-keepers?" Gandhi, *Collected Works* Vol. XC, 535.

pp. 129, 131, "Friends and comrades . . ." Nehru, *Jawaharlal Nehru's Speeches*, 151.

p. 131,   "India gave us Barrister Gandhi . . ." "Gandhi Film Kicks Off With Madiba's Speech," *Pretoria News* (South Africa), July 31, 2007.

BIBLIOGRAPHY

Arnold, David, and Stuart H. Blackburn, eds. *Telling Lives in India: Biography, Autobiography and Life History.* Bloomington, IN: Indiana University Press, 2004

The *Bhagavad Gita*, translated from the Sanskrit with an introduction by Juan Mascaro. Great Britain: Penguin Books, 1962.

Borra, Ranjan. "Subhas Chandra Bose, The Indian National Army, and the War of India's Liberation." *Journal of Historical Review* 4, no. 3 (Winter 1982).

Brittain, Vera. *Search After Sunrise.* London: Macmillan & Co., 1951.

Carroll, Ror. "Gandhi branded racist as Johannesburg honours freedom fighter." *Guardian* (UK), October 17, 2003.

Chadha, Yogesh. *Gandhi: A Life.* New York: John Wiley & Sons, 1997.

Demi. *Gandhi.* New York: Margaret K. McElderry, 2001.

Fischer, Louis. *The Life of Mahatma Gandhi.* London: Harper Collins, 1950.

Gandhi, Mahatma. *The Collected Works of Mahatma Gandhi.* Vol. I-XC. New Delhi: The Publications Division, 1958-1984.

―――. *The Essential Gandhi: An Anthology of His Writings on His Life, Work, and Ideas*, edited by Louis Fischer. New York: Vintage Books, 2002.

―――. *The Words of Gandhi, Selected by Richard Attenborough.* New York: Newmarket Press, 1982.

―――. *An Autobiography or The Story of My Experiments with Truth.* Translated by Mahadev Desai. Ahmedabad, India: Navajivan Publishing House, 1927.

Gandhi, Mohandas K. *Gandhi An Autobiography: The Story of My Experiments with Truth*, translated by Mahadev Desai. Boston: Beacon Press, 1957.

―――. *Non-Violent Resistance* (Satyagraha). Mineoloa, New York: Dover Publications, 2001.

―――. *Satyagraha in South Africa*, translated by Valji Govindji Desai. Ahmedabad: Navajivan Publishing House, 1928.

Grant, Joanne, ed. *Black Protest: History, Documents, and Analyses 1619 to Present.* New York: Fawcett World Library, 1968.

Green, Martin. *Tolstoy and Gandhi, Men of Peace.* New York: Basic Books, 1983.

Herman, Dr. Arthur. "Mahatma Gandhi: Warrior of Nonviolence." Lecture delivered on April 29, 2010. Smithsonian Institution, Washington, D.C.

Joshi, Pushpa, ed. *Gandhi on Women: Collection of Mahatma Gandhi's Writings and Speeches on Women*. Ahmedabad: Navajivan Publishing House, 1988.

Kala, Avind. "The Mahatma and his 'girls.'" *Free Press* (Mumbai, India) *Journal*, January 12, 1997.

Lapierre, Dominique, and Larry Collins. *Freedom at Midnight*. New Delhi: Vikas Publishing House, 1997.

Lewis, David L. *King: A Biography*. Urbana: University of Illinois Press, 1970.

Metcalf, Barbara D., and Thomas R. Metcalf. *A Concise History of India*. Cambridge: Cambridge University Press, 2002.

Mirabehn (Madeleine Slade). *Gandhi's Letters to a Disciple*. New York: Harper & Brothers, 1950.

Nehru, Jawaharlal. *Jawaharlal Nehru's Speeches*, vol. 1. Sept 1946-May 1949. New Delhi: Publications Division, 1949.

———. *Mahatma Gandhi*. Bombay: Asia Publishing House, 1949.

Pastan, Amy. *Gandhi*. New York: DK Publishing, 2006.

Reader's Digest Illustrated History of South Africa. The Real Story, 3rd ed. Cape Town, South Africa: The Reader's Digest Association South Africa, 1994.

Rolland, Romain. *Mahatma Gandhi: The Man Who Became One with the Universal Being*. Translated by Catherine D. Groth. New Delhi: Publications Division, 1924.

Sheehan, Vincent. *Lead, Kindly Light*. New York: Random House, 1949.

Thoreau, Henry David. "On Civil Disobedience." http://thoreau.eserver.org/civil.html

———. *Walden*. London: George Routledge & Sons, 1904.

Tolstoy, Leo. *The Kingdom of God Is Within You*. Translated by Leo Wiener. New York: Noonday Press, 1961.

———. Leo Nikolayevich. *Correspondence of Tolstoy*. Sydney, Australia: Accessible Publishing Systems, ReadHowYouWant Classics Library, 2008.

———. Letter to Gandhi. September 7, 1910. http://en.wikisource.org/wiki/Correspondence_between_Tolstoy_and_Gandhi

Trumbull, Robert. "Gandhi Is Killed by a Hindu." *New York Times*, January 31, 1948.

Wilkinson, Philip. *Gandhi: the young protester who founded a nation*. Washington, DC: National Geographic Children's Books, 2005.

WEB SITES

http://mkgandhi.org/

Includes research material on Gandhi, including photographs, writings, and a chronology. Information on nonviolence and conflict resolution is also available.

http://mahatma.com/

Features a timeline, research material, photographs, and famous speeches.

INDEX

PICTURE CREDITS

Cover:	Dinodia Photos / Alamy
13:	Dinodia Photos / Alamy
15:	Dinodia Photos / Alamy
16-17:	Mary Evans Picture Library / Alamy
19:	Courtesy of M.M.
26-27:	Courtesy of University of Houston Digital Library India Illustrated Frenzhcim Memorial Library Collection
31:	Courtesy of Library of Congress American Memory
34:	Dinodia Photos / Alamy
37:	Lebrecht Music & Arts/The Image Works
38-39:	Friedrich Stark / Alamy
42:	Dinodia Photos / Alamy
46:	Dinodia Photos / Alamy
51:	Lebrecht Music and Arts Photo Library / Alamy
52:	Dinodia Photos / Alamy
62:	The Art Archive / Alamy
66-67:	Dinodia Photos / Alamy
70-71:	Dinodia Photos / Alamy
76:	Dinodia Photos / Alamy
80:	Pep Roig / Alamy
87:	Dinodia Photos / Alamy
88-89:	Mary Evans Picture Library / Alamy
95:	Dinodia Photos / Alamy
102-103:	Dinodia Photos / Alamy
109:	Dinodia Photos / Alamy
114:	Dinodia Photos / Alamy
117:	Dinodia Photos / Alamy
118-119:	Courtesy of the United States Marine Corps
126:	Photos 12 / Alamy
130-131:	Dinodia Photos / Alamy